HOW TO SING

Luisa Tetrazzini

HOW TO SING

BY

LUISA TETRAZZINI

London

C. Arthur Pearson, Ltd.

Henrietta Street

1923

Printed in Great Britain at
The Mayflower Press, Plymouth. William Brendon & Son, Ltd.

CONTENTS

HOW TO SING

HOW TO SING

CHAPTER I

DON'T WAIT TO BE " FOUND "

EVERY day of my life I receive letters from men and women, mostly women, whom I do not know personally, asking me to advise them how best to use their vocal talents. Some of my correspondents also request me to give them an audition so that they can demonstrate their claim to be embryonic stars.

It is manifestly impossible for me to spend all my time listening to persons unknown to me, in the hope of finding new Carusos, new Pattis and, shall I say it ? —new Tetrazzinis. If I were to do so I should have little time for my own practice. Nevertheless, whenever I am able, I do give an audition to a young aspirant to musical fame, as I consider it my duty to help, to the best of my ability, those who are to come after me.

To those correspondents whom I have been unable to see personally let me say that star singers are not necessarily discovered by stars. It is quite true that

HOW TO SING

from time to time it has been my fortunate experience to discover a tenor or a baritone or a soprano. But they had already been more or less discovered before I found them.

True at Covent Garden I found John McCormack singing a very minor rôle and was instrumental in having him elevated to the position of principal tenor. And other *prime donne* have acted similarly.

Nevertheless these artists would doubtless have come to the front in their own time without being " discovered " by a *prima donna*. Most big artists of to-day were not found by anyone : they found themselves. I, for instance, was nobody's find. When the *prima donna* failed to appear at the opening night of an opera in my native Florence I volunteered to take the part, and in so doing discovered myself.

My readers will therefore understand that to be discovered by a great singer is not essential to becoming a great artist, and that because I am unable to give auditions to all who ask me I am not hindering them from becoming successful.

But for the benefit of those numerous correspondents who have expressed to me a desire that I should help all interested in training their voices, especially in their attempts to climb the difficult ladder of successful singing in public, I have consented to publish the following hints, and I hope sincerely they will be useful to all who read them.

I do not claim that I have given an exhaustive treatise—no one ever has done so—on the art of singing, but I am sure that anyone possessing a voice who cares to put into practice the suggestions I am now making, will be benefited thereby.

From this handbook I have purposely excluded the story of my professional life. That is already published under the title of " My Life of Song " (Cassell and Co., London ; Dorrance, Philadelphia, U.S.A.).

It will be observed that I use the word " he " all the way through when meaning " he or she." This is merely because I understand there is no English word which expresses the both. It would have been more modern to have used " she " in every case, but perhaps less modest. My lady readers will, however, understand that I am writing at least as much, if not more, for their benefit than for our lords and masters.

CHAPTER II

SINGERS may be divided into two classes. No, I do not mean, as some might suppose, those who can sing and those who cannot, though that is a possible classification. I mean in this case those who sing for mere pleasure and those who intend to make a career in this way. It is for both that these pages are intended.

As we have often been told, whatever is worth doing at all is worth doing well, and there is no reason why the singers who practise our beautiful art only for the enjoyment of themselves and their friends should not make the most of the powers which the good God has given them. I think, indeed, that it is their plain duty to do so, if only in the interests of their hearers. And I am glad to think that nowadays many see the matter in this light.

However it may be in the case of professional singers—upon which point I shall have something to say presently—there is, I suppose, no doubt that the standard of amateur singing has enormously improved during recent years.

The days when it was thought that anyone, however

YOUR AIM

poorly equipped, had the right to stand up and perform in public, have passed away, and in those circles, at all events, where there is any kind of pretension to general intelligence and culture it is expected that all who come forward in this way shall show themselves to be possessed of at least some knowledge of the rudiments of the art.

As to the general necessity for study on the part of those who aspire to sing, few words, I suppose, are necessary. If everyone can sing after a fashion, there is, I venture to say, no branch of the art of music which demands a more arduous apprenticeship and more prolonged study, if all of its higher possibilities are to be realised.

Precisely, however, because singing is in itself such a purely natural proceeding, this elementary fact is too often overlooked. " Singing," it has been well said, " derives its power from nature, but owes its perfection to art," and this is a fact which, I am afraid, is too often forgotten.

People, who would not dream of attempting to play the violin or give a piano solo in public without thorough preparation, will have no hesitation in standing up and attempting to sing, although they may be just as little qualified in the one case as in the other. They do not realise that the voice is, in reality, one of the most delicate and difficult of all instruments and demands in consequence no less study and practice than any other before it can be really artistically employed.

HOW TO SING

There is, moreover, another aspect of the singer's art which should never be forgotten. I allude to the fact that the singer is necessarily a reproductive artist —one whose business it is from the nature of the case to reproduce and interpret the music of others.

This imposes a duty and an obligation which should never be lost sight of. A singer has not only his own reputation to consider, but also that of the composer whose music he interprets, and for this reason alone, therefore, he can never take his art too seriously.

As to those contemplating a professional career, no words of mine will be necessary, I hope, to impress upon them the necessity of the sternest self-discipline and the most unremitting application if they are ever to succeed in accomplishing anything worth doing.

, CHAPTER III

WHY SINGERS ARE SCARCE

THE career of a singer is one offering a certain number of prizes but many, many blanks, and only those possessed of the most unmistakable natural gifts and ready to work tremendously hard should ever be encouraged to embark upon it. Hard work, beyond everything, is essential if success is to be achieved, and it is here, I am afraid, that so many of our modern students fail.

Imbued with the eager impatient spirit of these headlong days, they want to do things too quickly, and are unwilling to submit to the toil and drudgery which are none the less as necessary as ever if really solid results are to be achieved. It has even been suggested that to this circumstance may be traced that scarcity of great singers nowadays of which we hear so often.

True, more vocalists than ever before, probably, are inviting attention at the present time, but how few of them can be reckoned in the first class ? Doubtless it is easy to exaggerate in this matter. Seen through the mists of time the figures of the past always tend to assume heroic proportions.

HOW TO SING

Making due allowance, however, in this respect, are we really the victims of hallucination in thinking that great singers are fewer nowadays than formerly ? It would be pleasant to think so, but I am afraid that the facts point the other way.

What, then, is the explanation ? Different authorities would doubtless suggest different answers, but most, I fancy, would agree that lack of adequate study has had not a little to do with the matter.

Porpora, we all know, kept Caffarelli for five years to one page of exercises, and at the end of that time told him that he was the greatest singer in Europe. It would be amusing to learn the experience of a modern teacher who proposed to one of his pupils the adoption of the same course. The great Patti, who told me I was her successor, also said to me that we artists will still be learning when we are too old to sing.

The average vocal student of to-day considers himself a finished artist at a time when he would be reckoned just qualified to begin serious study by the teachers of an earlier period.

While no amount of training will make fine voices out of poor material, the history of singing furnishes numerous instances—that of Pasta is one of the best known—in which limited natural powers have been developed to an astonishing degree by study and training. Nowadays I am afraid it is the converse of this which is more frequently illustrated, and one hears only too often of fine natural voices which have been steadily ruined by the manner in which they are used.

Modern music has also, no doubt, had its influence —not so much because it is harmful to the voice in itself, but simply because it is possible to sing it (after a fashion) without such prolonged study and exercise as that of the older school absolutely necessitated.

Rossini, Donizetti, Bellini, and the rest of the old masters have indeed been avenged in a wholly unanticipated manner. Precisely as the music of their school has fallen in favour has the power been lost of singing that of the so-call'd higher kind which has taken its place.

CHAPTER IV

PERIOD OF TRAINING

FOR this melancholy state of affairs the only remedy is a return to sounder views. The fact must be recognised that there are no short cuts to perfection in singing any more than in any other art, and that those who wish to sing like the great ones of the past must be prepared to work and study as they did, in order to attain this end.

What period of training should be considered sufficient to equip a vocal student? In former days eight, nine, or even ten years were not considered too much for this purpose. I need hardly say how very different are the views prevailing nowadays, when students consider themselves qualified to appear in public at the end of a year or two's hasty and necessarily superficial training. Needless to say, no satisfactory results can possibly be achieved in this length of time. I consider a minimum of four years necessary to become a professional singer.

Lilli Lehmann has put the matter happily. At least six years, she says, should be considered the minimum period allowable—to which, she says further, there should then be added an entire life-time for further study and improvement !

This is not to say that many great singers have not perfected their art and even attained the very highest positions in a much shorter time. In my own case my period of actual systematic training in the strict sense of the term was comparatively brief—six months. But then in another sense I was learning from my childhood. Moreover, I was exceptionally lucky in that my voice was pitched just right, and had not to be trained to do what is usually regarded as difficult.

Almost from my infancy it was my ambition to become an operatic singer, and circumstances enabled me to benefit to the utmost extent by the constant hearing of opera, and also the constant criticism of singers by competent judges, so that I might be considered to have been studying and gaining experience for my after career all my life.

Most students, however, are not so fortunately situated, and for them I cannot urge too strongly the necessity of giving ample time to their studies if they hope to make the best of their powers and to establish their art on a firm foundation.

One can hardly write differently as to the period of training for the amateur than for the professional. If Patti said that she was still learning when she had retired from professional singing, no amateur can hope ever to have learned all there is to be known about the art of singing. And since he will always be a lover of song he will always be anxious to learn.

CHAPTER V

QUALITIES NEEDED

NEXT comes the question : What are the qualities which the vocal aspirant, professional or amateur, should possess ?

A famous teacher who was once asked this question made answer : " Voice ! Voice ! Voice ! " I agree, and in the case of the professional I should be inclined to add also : " Work ! Work ! Work ! " and then Faith, Hope, and Charity. Without hard work nothing can be done, and the practice of these three virtues will undoubtedly prevent one growing weary in his effort to attain the highest success.

But the truth is, of course, that many other qualities besides voice and industry are necessary here. There are, indeed, so many that I hardly know which to name first.

Lamperti on this point used to say : " First there must be a voice and good ear, but also an artistic soul and a musical disposition." Further, he used to insist upon sound judgment, deep conscientiousness in study, and untiring industry.

Very necessary also is general intelligence and keen perception, because no matter how good a teacher

QUALITIES NEEDED

may be the greater part of the work must be done through the brain of the student himself.

On the necessity of sound health it is hardly necessary to insist, while good looks and a fine presence naturally go for much also, though these are not absolutely indispensable, as many notable instances have gone to show.

Then, in addition, there are those temperamental qualities which mean so much : imagination and feeling, sympathy and insight, magnetism and personality. Perhaps, indeed, next to voice and ear these are the most important qualities of all. But unfortunately they cannot be acquired by any amount of study.

How often has it not happened, indeed, that artists have been endowed in all other respects but these ! They may have the most beautiful voices, they may sing with the most finished art, but for lack of these incommunicable attributes of the soul they never attain the highest places. They leave their audiences cold because they are cold themselves.

These are artists of the type which Lamperti used to refer to as mere " voice machines "—singers who, as Gounod once put it, are not artists at all in the true sense of the word, but merely people who " play upon the larynx," achieving great results perhaps in the purely vocal and mechanical sense, but never touching the hearts of their hearers for lack of those elemental human qualities which are essential if this result is to be attained.

HOW TO SING

Let the student do all in his power, therefore, to develop the higher side of his nature. By the study of literature and art, by the reading of fine poetry, by going to good plays, and in every other way let him cultivate his imagination and give play to his finer sensibilities.

For though such qualities as I have referred to may not be acquired when they are non-existent, they may be drawn out and developed if they are merely latent ; and in the case of members of the northern races especially this is not infrequently the case.

Another quality of a different kind which is none the less very valuable, indeed essential, is the power of self-criticism ; and I attach great importance also to having abundant faith in oneself. Even if it be pushed to the point of vanity and conceit—as I am afraid it occasionally is—this helps enormously when it is a case of withstanding the jolts and jars almost inseparable from the practice of vocal art.

CHAPTER VI

GENERAL CULTURE

OF course, too, wide general culture is very necessary. Everything that can be possibly acquired in this way helps, and is, indeed, almost more necessary to the singer than in the case of any other branch of the profession.

For the art of the singer is brought into immediate relation with all the other arts. The singer has to deal with poetry and literature and the drama—if he takes up opera—in a way quite unknown to the mere instrumentalist.

A man might be a great pianist or a fine violinist— he might even be a great composer—without ever concerning himself at all with the other arts. But in the case of the singer this would be quite impossible.

For it is the singer's business to interpret poetry in song and to play his part in drama on the stage, and it is obvious that he cannot hope to do these things properly without making himself acquainted with those arts also in addition to his own.

How can one hope, for instance, for a fine interpretation of a great song if the words themselves mean nothing to the singer ? He may sing the notes, but he cannot possibly do justice to his task unless he enters completely into the spirit of the words and the meaning of the poet.

And in the same way how can one hope to give a satisfactory impersonation of a part in an opera except by studying carefully the drama as a whole, grasping the intentions of the author, making oneself acquainted with the period of the action, and generally entering into it and all the literary, dramatic, historical, and other details of the work as well as considering it from the purely musical point of view ?

I am well aware that the opposite practice has often enough been followed. I have heard, indeed, of artists who have sung in such an opera as " Il Trovatore " for years without having ever troubled to understand the course of the action as a whole, and who were consequently in a state of total ignorance as to what it was all about.

But I cannot believe that anyone who addressed himself to his task in that unintelligent spirit would ever be likely to give an interpretation of his own part of much significance or value.

In my own case I go so far as to study not only, as a whole, any opera in which I have to take part, but even to learn, or at all events familiarise myself with, all of the other rôles. And I may add that I have found the practice helpful not only to myself but also to my fellow-artists before now, when perhaps some nervous tenor or timid débutante has temporarily " dried up," and I have been enabled to come to the rescue and relieve the situation.   This, however, merely *en passant*.

The main point I am insisting on for the moment is that the vocalist who wishes to make the most of his powers cannot have too solid a foundation in the way of general knowledge and culture.   There may be no direct connection between the one thing and the other, but his art will benefit none the less—will gain in depth and force and subtlety—in virtue of the fact that it is the outcome of a cultivated nature and the product of a mind which has thought and pondered over the deeper problems of existence.

CHAPTER VII

I MAY add, too, that there is no excuse for singers to neglect the cultivation of their minds, inasmuch as they have so much more time for this purpose than many of their fellow-students in other branches of the profession.

Thus, while a pianist or a violinist can, and indeed must, practice many hours a day, a singer cannot and should not do this, and therefore they have so much the more time available for the purpose of other study, including, I need hardly say, not only art and literature, but also the other branches of musical culture.

I know that singers have often been reproached in this matter and, I am afraid, not without good reason in earlier days, but I trust and believe that that time is passing away, and that vocalists nowadays are no longer looked upon as being necessarily lacking in general musical knowledge.

To which I need hardly add that many instances could be quoted of famous singers who are or have been admirably equipped also in other respects. The late Madame Sembrich was, for instance, a brilliant all-

26

STUDY AN INSTRUMENT

round musician who played both the piano and the violin with the ability of a professional. Madame Lilli Lehmann, still happily with us, although now advanced in years, is another whose accomplished art was based on fine general musicianship.

In point of fact the vocal student can hardly be too well equipped in the musical sense. He cannot hear too much good instrumental music ; he cannot be too well acquainted with the works of the great masters ; and, in short, cannot have too wide a basis of general musical knowledge as a foundation for his own specialised branch of the art.

To this end the study of an instrument is, of course, invaluable. The violin is an excellent instrument, though not so helpful from a vocal point of view as the piano. The piano naturally suggests itself as the most useful one for the purpose, since it helps directly in the pupil's vocal studies and makes him independent to some extent of an accompanist. It also gives every facility for obtaining a thorough knowledge of harmony.

It should be employed to further the service of general musical study on the lines above suggested.

Nor should the musical training of the vocalist stop at playing the piano, for he should know something of composition and general theory. A musical education is, indeed, almost indispensable to the singer of the present day if he is to deal successfully with difficult modern music.

In short, the days have gone by when a singer's

HOW TO SING

accomplishments were summed up in the familiar formula of " *Vox et praeterea nihil*," and he, or she, who expects to achieve a place in the front ranks at the present time must be prepared to use brains as well as vocal cords.

CHAPTER VIII

VOICE

NEXT comes the question of voice. That this is a fundamental requisite you will not expect me to tell you, although it may be noted, in passing, that some of the greatest singers have started comparatively ill-equipped in this respect —or apparently so.

Of Pasta, for instance, we read that her voice at the outset was heavy and strong, but unequal and very hard to manage. It is said, indeed, that she never to the end of her career succeeded in producing certain notes without some difficulty.

Yet, as the result of incessant study and practice, sometimes pursued in retirement for long periods, she gradually subdued her rebellious and intractable organ, and was eventually recognised as one of the very greatest singers of her time. Jenny Lind's voice at the outset was also very unmanageable.

I might even quote the case of Caruso himself as another example. Caruso was one of my greatest friends. But he gave little promise in his younger days of the wonderful career which was in store for him.

Thus we are told that among his fellow-students at

HOW TO SING

the Scuola Vergina he was known as " *Il tenore vento*,"
meaning a thin reedy tenor, and when he had com-
pleted his studies neither his master nor anyone else
had any expectation that he was going to do anything
out of the way.

Vergine even remarked humorously of him that if
there was any gold in his voice it could only be likened
to that at the bottom of the Tiber, inasmuch as it was
not worth drawing out. Little did he guess in those
days how much rich gold his unpromising pupil was
destined to draw in time out of his wonderful organ !

Nor did his earliest appearances impress outside
critics any more favourably. The general opinion was
that his voice was sympathetic in quality but rather
small, and that he himself was lacking in temperament.
Caruso lacking in temperament ! How odd it seems
to us who knew him later ! But that was the impression
which he produced at first.

All of which goes to show that it is not always easy
to say in the beginning how any given voice will turn
out in the end.

At the same time I do not wish to encourage the
belief that one should begin with a poor voice, or that
every mediocre student can hope, with study, to become
a Caruso. For this would certainly be a disastrous
notion to disseminate.

Such cases as Caruso's are indeed quite exceptional,
and in the ordinary way a pupil can take it that if his
voice shows no promise at the outset he is not likely to
do very much with it later.

VOICE

On the other hand, what does happen only too frequently, as I have suggested before, is that a pupil starts with a fine voice which, however, through faulty training, want of application, or some other cause, eventually comes to nothing ; and it is this which is to be most carefully guarded against.

Sad it is, indeed, to think of the fine voices which have been lost to the world in this way ! Nor need one look very far for instances. Hardly a day passes, indeed, but what one reads or hears of some wonderful voice which has been " discovered " in this place or that. Alas ! how few of these wonderful voices eventually justify the hopes which they have aroused ! Either the other necessary qualities are lacking, or— too often, I am afraid—their training is entrusted to the wrong hands and they come to nothing.

CHAPTER IX

AS to the absolute necessity of a teacher there can, I suppose, hardly be two opinions. Much can be learnt from books, no doubt ; by listening to other singers ; and by working things out for oneself, so far as possible. Also it is a fact, doubtless, that some of the world's greatest singers have had remarkably little formal instruction.

Mario, for instance, never had a lesson in his life, except when Meyerbeer taught him the part of Raymond in " Robert le Diable "—and Meyerbeer, it is hardly necessary to say, was not a singing master.

But such cases are the exceptions, and in the ordinary way there cannot be the slightest doubt that the services of a teacher are absolutely essential to sound progress. There are exceptions, of course. One of these is the great Chaliapine, who represents his own school and has never had any instruction as we understand it. He is by nature endowed with a beautiful voice, and obtains his fine effects by long hours of deep thought and reflection. I have asked him when and how he prepares, and he replied : " I think out my work in the silence of my bedchamber, when I am waiting for sleep, or in the mornings before I rise. In fact, during all my hours of wakefulness I am always visualising the stage, the actors, the audiences, and contriving how best to obtain effects emotional, sentimental, dramatic."

Grave indeed are the risks run by any student who attempts to supply his own requirements in this matter and to dispense with the skilled advice which only the trained expert can supply—entailing possibly the ruin of his entire career.

It was for lack of such advice in her earlier days that Jenny Lind's voice was almost ruined at the outset, so that when she went to Garcia for advice his verdict was : " It is quite useless for me to think of teaching you, since you have no voice left."

Fortunately rest and proper training saved the situation in that case, as we all know, but how easily it might have been otherwise. Other fine voices have, indeed, been irretrievably destroyed by faulty methods continued too long.

A famous case was that of Duprez, a well-known tenor who flourished some seventy or eighty years ago. " I have lost my voice," he wrote in despair to Rubini, " how have you kept your's ? " Rubini replied : " My dear Duprez, you have lost your voice because you have sung with your capital ; I have kept mine because I have sung only with the interest." And there is a world of instruction in this pithy way of putting it.

See to it at all costs, therefore, that you put yourself

in the right hands. By which I do not necessarily mean a teacher of world-wide repute—for there are many equally good who do not happen to be so generally known. The supremely important thing is that whoever you go to shall be a man—or a woman, as the case may be—of honour and integrity, who can be trusted to deal faithfully with you, and not a quack or a charlatan.

The teaching of singing is indeed a much simpler matter—though difficult enough—than is commonly supposed, especially nowadays when, as the result of scientific study and research, the underlying physiological principles are so much more thoroughly understood than formerly. Yet there will always be those, I suppose, who find it to their advantage to deal with it as something mysterious and occult ; and apparently there will always be those confiding souls willing to take these folk at their own valuation and to put good money into their pockets.

Wonderful indeed are the tales which are told of some of these gentry. In New York, for instance, there is said to be a practitioner of this type who sells to his pupils, in order to give timbre to their voices, bottles (at 2 dollars each) of Italian water. Beware of the confidence tricksters of the musical profession who claim to transform your voice by some quack method or theory of " nasal resonance " and so on. These people have ruined more voices than one could enumerate.

But one need not go to America to find examples.

GOOD AND BAD "MAESTRI"

I am afraid, indeed, that even in my own native land the same sort of thing is not entirely unknown. I have even heard of a teacher in Milan who makes his pupils swear on a crucifix not to reveal the secret of his wonderful "method," and I have heard of another whose practice it was to make his pupils tie to the legs of the piano pieces of elastic which they were instructed to pull out and let go again, in order to "feel" the gradations of *crescendo* and *diminuendo*.

But even he seems to have been excelled in invention by another "Professor"—again hailing from the Land of the Stars and Stripes!—whose custom it was to illustrate the art of *mezza voce* by means of an umbrella which he opened and closed as his happy pupils, standing before him, swelled and diminished on the chosen note.

Such things, you may say, sound laughable enough, but they are no laughing matter for the unfortunate pupils who happened to be the victims of such monstrous quackery, and I cannot urge too earnestly upon all my readers the supreme importance of choosing a teacher who is above all suspicion—for preference one possessed of a satisfactory diploma obtained at a recognised institution.

Then you may be sure that whether the teacher be better or worse in the purely technical sense, he will at least be an honest man and not one who makes his calling a mere pretext for the plundering of the ignorant and unwary.

HOW TO SING

Another important question which arises in this connection is as to the advisability of studying at home or abroad, and this, I am afraid, is one of those perplexing matters in the case of which there is a good deal to be said on both sides. I myself have naturally a prejudice in favour of my beloved Italy, the traditional Land of Song, where, I am proud to think, the art of Bel Canto still finds its finest exponents and teachers, and where also there are greater facilities, I suppose, for hearing fine singing than in any other country in the world.

At the same time I am quite prepared to admit that there is a good deal to be said on the other side. It is a great undertaking and responsibility, for instance, sending a young girl to study abroad. The teacher selected may not be a good one, or may not be suited to her particular requirements, when she gets there— although by saying this I do not mean to express agreement with those who contend that a special kind of teaching is required for the singers of every nationality. Whether you study at home or abroad, let your teacher be the best you can obtain.

CHAPTER X

COMPASS AND QUALITY

HAVING found your teacher, the next thing you will want to know is precisely what sort of voice you have—and this is a matter, curiously enough, which cannot always be determined off-hand. The strangest mistakes have, indeed, not infrequently been made in this respect—as in the well-known instance of Jean de Reszke, who actually began his public career as a baritone and continued singing for some years before he finally came to the conclusion that his voice was, in reality, a tenor.

The important task of discovering whether a voice is bass, baritone, tenor, contralto, mezzo-soprano, or soprano, and the exact character of the general ranges of these voices is a matter of great delicacy, and cannot be decided at one hearing. It is largely individual, and sometimes a matter of health and circumstances. The ranges of different classes of the human voice may be generally stated as follows. In the bass voice two octaves of E, the contralto two octaves of E with a tone and a half more in the upper notes leading to G ; the tenor, which sounds an octave lower than the

37

HOW TO SING

soprano, and the soprano voice itself two octaves of C. There are also the baritone and mezzo-soprano voices, the former of which is neither bass nor tenor, and the latter neither contralto nor soprano. The average range covers two octaves of G or A in baritones and mezzo-sopranos.

In all cases there are, of course, exceptions, as, for example, the bass that extends to a melodious low C and can even reach the baritone top F. There is a further classification which has relation to the *timbre* or colour, which distinguishes whether the artist is dramatic or purely lyric. If of a lyric tendency the artist will do well to avoid dramatic declamation until maturity and experience has taught him this difficult side of our art and *vice versa.*

It is not a question of compass only, but of compass in addition to the distinctive character and quality of the voice. But compass is undoubtedly essential, and in regard to this Lamperti's practice was to judge not only by the notes which could be taken, but by the facility with which words could be enunciated on them at the same time.

Thus, in the case of a girl student, if she could not only sing the upper G, but could also enunciate words easily on that note, he considered that she was a true soprano ; and so on with all the other voices. Thus a baritone might be able to take notes almost as high as a tenor. But if he could not pronounce words comfortably on those notes he was not, in Lamperti's judgment, to be classed as anything but as baritone.

COMPASS AND QUALITY

But, as a general rule, your teacher will not have much difficulty in deciding as to the classification of your voice, and presuming this to have been decided we must consider next the question of training it.

Here I feel that I must go carefully, for if there is one thing more certain than another, in my opinion, it is that the pupil who hopes to get the best results from his training must place himself unreservedly in his teacher's hands, since otherwise he cannot possibly hope to do justice to his teaching. That is to say, he should not confuse his mind by accepting the advice and instruction of other people—so far, at all events, as concerns what may be called the strictly technical side of his training.

Therefore, I shall confine myself to general hints and observations only, based on my own experiences and herewith offered for what they are worth.

CHAPTER XI

AGE TO START TRAINING

AS to the age to start training the voice, this depends to some extent upon the individual, but speaking generally it may be said that in the case of boys the voice matures at about the age of from fourteen to sixteen, and that no serious work should be undertaken until after this period. Although choir-singing for boys affords wonderful training—in some cases, at all events, if not in all—it should not be persisted in too long.

If boys are allowed to sing on in the choir until their voices change, they may easily find, finally, that they have totally ruined their vocal organs for the rest of their lives. The utmost caution should be exercised, therefore, in this matter, and it should be the duty of every choirmaster to see that none of his choristers are permitted to run this grave risk by continuing their services too long.

In the case of girls, teaching may begin about the age of sixteen or seventeen, but not much earlier.

CHAPTER XII

ANATOMY AND PHYSIOLOGY

TO what extent a vocal student should be instructed in matters anatomical and physiological is a question which has often been raised, and upon which the most contradictory views have been expressed. It is argued by some, that having in mind all the great singers of the past who flourished before the laryngoscope was thought of, the less the student knows about such things the better. It is contended that he will surely become self-conscious and unnatural by thinking about the physiological mechanism of processes which should be absolutely instinctive and automatic ; and possibly in some instances this does occur.

I do not think, however, that if the instruction is properly given it need have any such effect, and I thoroughly believe, myself, in the student being given at least a general idea as to the construction of the vocal organs and the manner in which they function.

To precisely what extent the student should be instructed in what a famous singer once humorously

HOW TO SING

referred to as " thoracic, crico-thyroideal, and epiglottic matters " may be a question for consideration, but as to the desirability of his being acquainted in a general way with the working of the vocal apparatus I have no sort of doubt.

The truth is that the whole business of singing, if reduced to its elements, is much simpler and easier to understand than is sometimes supposed, and there is not the slightest reason why any difficulty need be experienced in explaining the matter in its general outlines. I would go further, indeed, and say that he is not likely to prove a very intelligent pupil who is not sufficiently curious and interested to wish to know something upon the subject.

At the same time, it is, no doubt, perfectly true that many of the greatest singers of the past have been destitute of the slightest knowledge of such matters. In which connection one may recall the famous saying of Patti when interrogated as to her method : " Je n'en sais rien." But it does not follow that others not possessed of her marvellous natural gifts should follow her example in this respect. For she did unconsciously and instinctively what in the case of most others only comes as the result of laborious study and practice.

One may recall, in this connection, the saying of that profound student of the art on the technical side, who was also in her day such a great executant, Lilli Lehmann, that it is not enough to sing well. One must be told also the how and why, and be given a

ANATOMY AND PHYSIOLOGY

firm foundation, if permanent results are to be hoped for. For otherwise one will run the risk of coming to grief when for some reason or other an unexpected strain is put upon one's resources and there is no

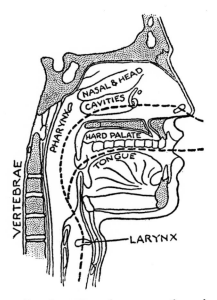

Rough section of nose, mouth, and pharynx, suggesting by dotted lines how the tone passes from the larynx through the mouth and passages of the head.

sound knowledge and understanding to fall back upon.

How can one properly understand, for instance, the all-important subject of breathing, if one has not at least some idea as to the natural processes involved ? Vocal teachers and students of voice production are often twitted upon the conflicting character of the

HOW TO SING

views which they hold and the principles which they lay down, but here is one subject, at all events, upon which there is universal agreement, namely, the supreme importance of right breathing as the very foundation of the singer's art.

CHAPTER XIII

BREATHING

HE who breathes properly sings properly, it has been said ; and there is not a single authority of any weight, I venture to say, who does not endorse that statement. The old Italian masters used to say, indeed, that the art of singing *is* the art of breathing ; and the same idea was put by Lamperti in another way when he observed that " the attainment of proper respiration should be the first object of the student of singing."

On the same subject the words of a famous English singing teacher, William Shakespeare, may be quoted. In his well-known work on the Art of Song he lays down as the two fundamental aims to be set before himself by the student : 1, how to take a breath and how to press it out slowly ; and, 2, how to sing to this controlled breath pressure.

It is when we come to consider the views of the different theorists in detail that divergencies will be found to arise. But on certain fundamental matters there will, I think, be found pretty general agreement nowadays.

The great guiding principle to be borne in mind, in

HOW TO SING

my opinion, is ease and naturalness. This is one of those matters in regard to which nature can be trusted much more safely than theorists and professors. I refer, of course, to the actual process of breathing. As regards the subsequent production of tone there is, of course, plenty to be taught. But the actual process of

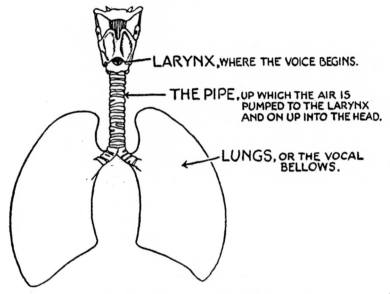

LARYNX, WHERE THE VOICE BEGINS.

THE PIPE, UP WHICH THE AIR IS PUMPED TO THE LARYNX AND ON UP INTO THE HEAD.

LUNGS, OR THE VOCAL BELLOWS.

Rough diagram of the larynx, trachea and lungs.

inspiration and exhalation should be as natural and as easy as possible.

Some wise words of Salvatore Marchesi may be quoted on this point : " When explaining the physical, mechanical process of breathing to beginners it is essential to make them understand that natural laws have provided for its independence of our will, as is

46

BREATHING

observed in sleeping. Therefore, every intentional preparation or effort made in order to draw more air into the lungs will produce the contrary result, hindering the freedom of the natural process."

But this is not to imply that breathing capacity cannot be cultivated and developed by practice. On the contrary, a vast amount can be done in this way, just as in the case of any other organ of the body, by means of systematic exercise and practice. Everyone has heard, for instance, of the wonderful way in which the breathing capacity of native divers in the tropics is developed in the course of their calling, or of that old man in the Bay of Naples who stops under the water with a watch in hand for 35 seconds. Singers can acquire something of the same power, and must do so, indeed, if they hope ever to achieve the best results. For the production of good sustained tone is impossible if the art of breathing is not properly understood and acquired.

Among modern singers no one attached more importance to breathing and breath control than the late Signor Caruso, and no one, certainly, attained more wonderful results in this way. He developed his powers to such an extent indeed in this respect, that it was said that he could move a grand piano by the expansion of the muscles of his diaphragm! And whether this be true or not it is certain that his wonderful breathing capacity was, as he himself used to declare, in large measure the secret of his consummate art.

47

HOW TO SING

Try to avoid breathing through the mouth. Inhalation through the nostrils purifies and warms the air before it reaches the throat. Breathing through the mouth dries the throat and makes the voice husky. Nevertheless, in singing declamatory music what are called half breaths through the mouth are necessary.

When practising avoid taking sudden breaths, though this may also be necessary when performing publicly.

Practice once daily before a looking-glass and so correct faults of breathing and grimaces.

Don't heave the shoulders when taking breath. There should be no visible movement of the body.

When practising breathing—and this should be done every day—inhale a long slow breath to the full lung capacity, hold for one or two seconds, and then exhaust in the same slow gentle way. This is rather exhausting, and two or three periods of five minutes with an interval of say fifteen minutes should be sufficient for each day.

CHAPTER XIV

BUT, of course, breathing alone is not sufficient. After the breathing capacity has been developed the power thus acquired must be rightly applied, and here the first principle is right emission, and in particular the rule that the release of the breath and the attack of the tone must take place simultaneously. In other words, no breath at all must be permitted to escape before the production of tone.

It is to attain this result that the so-called *coup de glotte*, or " shock of the glottis," has been advocated. To appreciate this term it is necessary to understand exactly how vocal tone is produced.

I will not attempt to go into the matter fully, but the general principles involved are quite easily grasped.

Taken broadly, then, it will be understood that vocal sound is produced by a column of air passing from the lungs through a small aperture formed by the vocal cords within the larynx (see diagrams). When we breathe in the ordinary way the air passes in and out as we inspire and exhale, without any sound being produced. This is because the passage through the larynx is then quite clear. No obstruction is

D   49

offered to the air current, and in consequence the process is quite noiseless.

When, however, we wish to utter a sound, Nature provides for this by enabling us to interpose an obstruction to the air current by means of the vocal cords, and the air then has to pass through a small slit or aperture, sometimes called the " vocal chink," formed by their being drawn closely together curtain-wise, as it were.

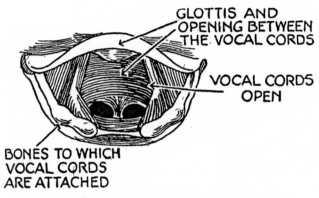

The vocal cords during deep breathing.

When the vocal cords—or ligaments, as they are perhaps better described—are drawn together in this manner the passage of the air is so restricted that it can only pass in short rapid pulsations, instead of, as before, in a continuous stream, and the result of these pulses or vibrations is the production of sound or tone.

The aperture, or chink, is called the glottis, and the character of the tone resulting, in particular the pitch

VOCAL CORDS

of it, is regulated by the precise disposition and proximity to one another of the two bands or cords or ligaments—sometimes they are known as the vocal lips —by which the chink or opening is formed.

The process itself of regulating the opening of the vocal cords in this way is entirely automatic and subconscious. We merely *will* to produce a tone of a certain pitch and the vocal cords automatically, and without any conscious effort on our part, are brought together to precisely the right degree necessary to produce that particular tone.

The vocal cords during the singing of a high note.

From this it will be understood that every note that is uttered, every inflection even of the speaking voice, however minute, requires a slightly different adjustment of these infinitely delicate threadlike membranes which are provided for this purpose within the boxlike larynx ; and this extraordinarily delicate adjustment is all effected quite automatically and instinctively by the mere operations of the will.

The brain intimates, so to speak, that it requires a certain note to be produced and forthwith, without

51

the slightest conscious act of adjustment on the part of the singer or speaker, the vocal ligaments adapt themselves precisely in the manner required and the particular note desired is duly produced.

And these notes may issue forth through that tiny aperture and from the throat of the singer to the number of a dozen or more in a second—each one requiring a separate adjustment of the aperture and the said adjustment being effected in every instance, in the case of a properly trained singer, absolutely perfectly and exactly.

Surely of all the many wonderful contrivances which go to the making of the mechanism of the human body there is none which is more wonderful than this ! It is, indeed, necessary only to consider the elaboration of the means and the complexity of the muscular adjustments necessary to achieve similar results in the case of a violin, say, or a piano, in order to realise the amazing ingenuity and efficiency of the means employed by Nature.

But I am wandering from the *coup de glotte*, which I set out to explain. Let it be understood, therefore, that the *coup de glotte* is merely a name for a particular method of bringing together the lips of the vocal cords, and certain subordinate muscles known as the ventricular bands, with a view to a better and cleaner production of tone, and with a view especially to the avoidance of the particular fault above referred to, namely, the emission of air before the production of the note.

VOCAL CORDS

In the result the " attack " is certainly very sharp and clean, but personally I cannot recommend this particular method of achieving that result, since the effect is anything but agreeable to the ear, and there is good reason for thinking that the practice, besides being unnecessary, is also injurious to a vocal organ.

I will not go further into the matter, however, since all such technical details are for the teacher to explain and illustrate and cannot be satisfactorily dealt with in print.

Certain general principles may, however, be touched on, amongst which the first is, perhaps, that there should never be at any time the smallest conscious strain or effort. Relaxation, looseness, ease, should be the watchwords all the time. Rigidity, tightening of the muscles, stiffness, contraction, are fatal to the production of beautiful tone. Here, as so often in art, when grace and beauty are the objects aimed at, economy of effort is the grand secret.

There should never be any strain or forcing of any sort or kind, and on the same principle, it may be noted, is the rule as to the amount of breath emitted, which should always be the smallest quantity possible which suffices to produce the tone required. Let out enough breath and no more—keeping the remainder in reserve—that is one of the fundamental secrets of beautiful tone production.

Lilli Lehmann puts the same point in another way when she insists on the supreme importance of emitting " as little breath as possible." Perhaps I may be permitted to quote, also, in this connection some interesting remarks of Signor Salvatore Fugito, in a recently published volume, in reference to the practice of Caruso in this regard.

" Caruso governed the expiratory flow of the breath with such mastery that not a particle of it escaped without giving up its necessary equivalent in tone. Caruso emitted for each musical phrase, or for each note, just enough breath to produce that phrase or note musically and *no more*. The remaining breath he kept in reserve, which made the enchanted hearer feel that the master was still far from the limit of his resources, that he had still ample motive power in reserve for whatever the occasion might require."

Another great master of breathing is Battistini. One hears him singing long phrases, one after the other, without perceiving when or how he fills his lungs, so completely has he covered up all traces of the physical effort. There is no puffing and panting, no discoloration or distortion of the face.

I am myself often asked how I manage to find the breath for the long florid passages which I so often have to sing, and my reply usually is that I have a good pair of bellows which I make a point of always keeping well filled with air.

This can be done, I may add, in the case of such passages as I have mentioned by taking at times only partial breaths instead of full ones. These can naturally be taken much more quickly than complete inspirations,

VOCAL CORDS

and by their means the " bellows " can be kept constantly replenished even when the heaviest demands are being made upon their contents.

But while it is essential to maintain a good pressure of air behind the tone, this does not mean that the lungs must be filled to distention, for this produces the worst possible result. Madame Lilli Lehmann has recorded, for instance, in her valuable treatise on singing, that she made this mistake in the first instance, with the result that she always felt as if she must release some of her superfluous breath before beginning to sing.

" Undoubtedly," she writes, " I took in too much air in breathing and cramped various muscles, thereby depriving my breathing organs and muscles of their elasticity. I often had, with all my care and preparation for inhalation, too little breath, and sometimes, when not giving special thought to it, more than enough." And others not infrequently commit the same error under the mistaken impression that they must get as much air into their lungs as possible.

CHAPTER XV

A N all-important part of the student's training is that in relation to what is called the " placing " of the voice. This somewhat vague term has been the subject of a good deal of misunderstanding, and the most curious notions have gained currency as to its actual meaning. Yet this is, in reality, quite simple.

Tone is made in the first instance, as I have already explained, by the breath passing through the vocal cords. The precise *quality* of the tone depends, however, on the formation and disposition of the various parts of the vocal apparatus—throat, palate, tongue, and so on—through which the breath afterwards passes before issuing from the mouth.

The disposition of these various parts can be varied by the individual, and the placing of the voice consists in finding how best to adjust them in order to get the most satisfactory tone, and in acquiring the power always to produce tone in this way and in no other.

To assist in attaining this result it is usual to instruct the pupil to sing " forward," " dans le masque," and so on, but it should be clearly understood that though such terms are useful from the practical point of view, they are none the less only a *façon de parler*, and a means of instructing the pupil how to adjust and adapt the whole vocal apparatus, so to speak, in the most effective way.

You can really produce a tone in your face or in your throat. It is all produced by the vocal cords, and nowhere else, and merely receives its specific quality or character, so to speak, by, in part, the natural formation, and, in part, the conscious adjustment of the passages through which it passes on its way to the mouth.

But by thinking of the face or the throat and, so to speak, *apparently* fixing it there, you can modify the disposition of the various parts in question and so influence the quality of the tone produced. This mysterious placing of the voice means, therefore, in reality, nothing more than finding out in each individual instance the best position of the vocal organs for getting the best results.

This, again, is one of those matters in regard to which little help can be derived from advice in books. Only by direct instruction from a capable master can a pupil possibly be made to understand completely what is required in this respect.

It is, indeed, essentially one of those matters in the case of which an ounce of practice and example is worth a ton of theory, and happy is the student who has the good fortune to go to a master capable of instructing him rightly on the point.

HOW TO SING

Some fortunate ones, like myself, have voices which are quite perfectly placed by Nature. That is to say, they are the lucky possessors of voices which they produce naturally and unconsciously in the most advantageous manner, so that they require to make no alteration at all.

This will, of course, be perceived at once by a capable master, who will be only too careful in such cases to leave well alone. A charlatan or impostor, on the other hand, can work irremediable harm by interfering with such voices and attempting to modify or improve them.

A singer with a perfect light soprano voice may, for instance, have the misfortune to fall into the hands of such a teacher, who will persuade her that she can sing the rôles of a dramatic soprano, and by misguided advice and training succeed in ruining a beautiful natural voice in the attempt to improve it.

In the vast majority of cases, however, the pupil's voice is not naturally placed so as to give the best results. That is to say, by proper instruction and training it can be made to produce better results—tones more smooth, more round, more resonant, and so on—and it is here that the services of an experienced and capable teacher are beyond price. The problem is one of great complexity, for so many different factors enter into it. The palate, the tongue, the teeth, the lips, as well as the natural and unalterable formation of the throat, and so forth, all play their part in determining the issue, and the slightest modifications in any

PLACING THE VOICE

one may easily effect the greatest differences in the results.

It is easy to understand, therefore, how impossible it is to lay down any general rules in the matter, but it is perhaps safe to say that the less the pupil is called upon to depart from his, or her, natural and instinctive procedure, the more likely are good results to be achieved—the ideal case being, of course, the one in which no alterations whatsoever are required.

I may add, perhaps, that some authorities attach great importance in this connection to the language used by the pupil in the earlier stages of his training— that is, when his voice is undergoing the process of being placed. That accomplished singer Signor Bonci is, for instance, one who holds strong views on this point.

According to him it is very injurious for singers at this stage of their studies to sing in more than one language. I may perhaps venture to quote what he has written on the subject : " When a tone is properly placed the word need not affect it, but a great deal of harm is caused by applying the word too early and beyond this by using several languages. It is a question, and a serious one, whether those who teach singing understand the application of the word to the tone, and the dangers are obvious in languages where nasals and gutturals prevail.

CHAPTER XVI

REGISTERS

CLOSELY allied with the question of " placing " is that of Registers, which has been the subject of so much controversy at various times. There is not even agreement as to how many registers there are—or even if there are any at all.

For while some take the view that there are no such things, others speak variously of two, three, four, and even more natural and inevitable divisions in the range of the average voice which can only be properly distinguished from one another in this way.

Some, I believe, even maintain that each individual note should properly be regarded as a different register. But this suggestion I think can scarcely be intended seriously. For if each individual note really does constitute a separate register, what is gained by talking of registers at all ?

There is, however, no denying that there are certain marked differences in the case of every voice in the quality of the tone produced at different parts of its range or compass—differences of tone quality which are accompanied also by different sensations on the part of the singer ; and to these different sections

REGISTERS

of the vocal range the name of registers has been given.

Usually three are recognised—chest, medium, and head, the term chest register being applied to the lowest notes, medium to the middle portion, and head to the highest.

The terms chest, medium, and head are derived from the sensations experienced by the singer in producing the different notes referred to—the lower ones giving the feeling of having been produced in the chest, the middle ones in the throat, and the highest ones of all in the head. But it should be understood that in actual fact there is no difference in the manner in which the various notes are produced.

All the notes of the voice, whether high or low, are in reality produced in the same way, namely, in the manner already described—by the passage of the air from the lungs through the " chink " formed by the vocal cords. In the case of the lower notes, however, owing to certain physiological causes, the vibrations are felt by the singer most strongly in and about the chest, and in the case of the higher ones in the head— whence, therefore, the somewhat misleading terms in use have been adopted.

At the same time the fact that these different sensations are experienced by the singer may be taken as the best possible evidence of the fact that there are definite differences in the method of tone production to account for them ; and this view of the matter is in fact confirmed by the researches of physiologists.

HOW TO SING

There is no need, of course, for vocalists to concern themselves with the matter in detail, for the process involved is, of course, entirely (or almost entirely) automatic. But it is none the less explained by the physiologists quite clearly why there is, at a certain point, this difference of feeling on the part of the singer in passing from the lower notes to the higher ones.

Without going too minutely into the matter, the reason broadly stated is that the vocal cords are differently disposed in the two cases. Up to a certain point the successive tones are produced in one uniform way, and then above that point the method is modified ; and it is this difference accordingly which is accountable for the distinctive sensations experienced by the singer—sensations, it may be added, which have been recognised and discussed ever since the art of singing has been studied.

Hence, it is quite a mistake to suggest, as has been done by some, that the whole notion of registers is a delusion. These different registers do undoubtedly exist, and it becomes one of the most important problems consequently to get rid of the " break," or change in the tone quality, which occurs when the voice passes from one to the other. At the same time it does not follow that violent and artificial methods should be adopted for this purpose.

On the contrary, little else than steady and properly directed practice is required in the ordinary way to accomplish this. In fact if you get your breathing

REGISTERS

right and your tone production in general right, the register difficulty will probably solve itself. To put it in another way, if you ensure that each individual tone is right, the problem of the registers need not seriously trouble you ; and this is a matter of paying attention to the general rules of sound tone production.

Special exercises are, however, usually given for the purpose of " equalising " the voice, as it is called, that is to say, for the purpose of ensuring a perfectly even and uniform quality of tone throughout the scale and avoiding the break at the change of register which has been referred to ; and these exercises are no doubt useful.

Most of the best authorities are agreed that proper breathing has as much to do with the matter as anything, some even going so far as to say that the matter should not be mentioned to the student at all. This is perhaps a somewhat extreme statement, but the underlying principle is sound. And here, as always, the principle of absolute ease and relaxation and the avoidance of all unnatural muscular contraction or violent effort is at once all important.

The following is generally conceded to be a well

thought out method of uniting the voice wherever the " break " occurs.

Sing this passage, *Messa di Voce*, ascending and

63

descending, commencing where the break is first noticeable. If this is practised consistently for two or three periods of twenty minutes a day it should be effective in preventing this unpleasant defect. Begin firmly, using " ay," " oh," or " ee," and swell out to fullest capacity. Then let the tone die away imperceptibly and be careful not to use falsetto. By doing the foregoing we have augmented the head tones to such an extent that instead of having falsetto, we have a head voice capable of being allied to the chest voice with practically no distinguishable break in the whole compass.

Contraltos are the greatest sinners with the " break." Very few contraltos are able to change the registers or sing two octaves without a perceptible gap. At one time this vulgar habit was considered a virtue when in reality it is a clear indication of lack of study and practice.

Remember that no matter where the " break " occurs it is only by cultivating the head voice that a cure can be attained.

Then, again, almost everybody has one or two tones more or less defective, and wherever these occur special attention must be given them so that they can be built up until the singer can safely overcome the " break."

CHAPTER XVII

FAULTS

A FEW words on faults—and the correction of them. No, I am not going to attempt a catalogue of all the faults which are possible, but name just a few : faulty intonation ; faulty phrasing ; imperfectly attacking notes ; " scooping " up to notes ; " digging " or arriving at a note from a semitone beneath it ; singing off the key or out of tune and tremolo. All of these faults are unforgivable, but the last two are crimes. And I could name numbers more. I have heard vocalists who have been horrified when I told them that they arrived at a note after attacking it from a fourth below, especially when singing *pianissimo*. Consequently I cannot over emphasise the supreme need for the student to recognise his faults and follies if he hopes ever to make progress.

Nay, this is not putting it strongly enough. He should not merely be ready to recognise his faults, but eager to discover them. He should be ever on the look out to realise his deficiencies and to regard as his best friends those who are kind enough to tell him of them.

HOW TO SING

This may sound self-obvious, but I am afraid that in practice the attitude of the average student—and not of the student only, but also of the experienced artist—is very different. A fatal self-satisfaction seems, for some reason or other, to be one of the commonest failings of the average singer. One fairly well-known singer invited my criticism of her voice, and when I obliged and told her what she must do to become a great artist she replied, " But I am a great artist." At which I bowed and said, " I beg your pardon, madam."

Yet it is hardly necessary to say—we can all realise it indeed in the case of others—that there is no form of weakness more absolutely fatal to artistic progress. Let the student beware, therefore, against this dangerous form of vanity and self-sufficiency, and learn from all who can teach him.

How often have I not heard of students—alike young and old—who have been foolish enough to throw over good teachers because they have been honest enough and courageous enough to tell them unpalatable truths ! They think they know better. They are so supremely well pleased with themselves—so foolishly satisfied with their own achievements—that they regard it as an offence when their errors are pointed out.

Of course they do not put it—even to themselves— in this way. They prefer to persuade themselves that their teacher is at fault. They explain that they do not like his " method." Or they say that he does not " understand " their particular voice. And so they

66

FAULTS

come to the conclusion that they had better make a change and go to some other master instead.

It is all very human but very foolish, and I cannot impress this too strongly upon all who read this book. Your best friend is one who will tell you faithfully, not how beautifully you sing, but how badly !

Some are, of course, wise enough to realise this. And you will generally find that they are the ones who get on. Such a one was Caruso, who, to the end of his day, never ceased to practice, to study, to reflect upon his art, and even to worry and agitate himself over his supposed deficiencies—deficiencies which were unperceived by his hearers but which he, with his fastidious and ultra-sensitive artistic conscience, persuaded himself were there.

CHAPTER XVIII

COLORATURA SINGING

I SUPPOSE there is no question which I am more frequently asked by vocal students and others interested than how to acquire agility, but I am afraid my answer is usually disappointing. For I can only repeat that it is simply a case of perseverance and hard work, plus, of course, whatever natural abilities in that direction you may possess.

It is obvious that all singers are not equally endowed in this respect. The mere fact that there is such a difference in this matter between the various classes of voices is sufficient to prove that. No one ever expects a contralto voice to have the same facility in this regard as a light soprano, and still less a bass or a baritone.

The most unceasing practice would never have enabled an Alboni or a Lablache, say, to achieve the dazzling runs and fioriture of a Patti or a Catalani. And to a less marked degree there are similar differences between individual voices of the same class. All are not equally capable in this particular even when in other respects they may be equally good.

Some experienced teachers indeed recognise this

COLORATURA SINGING

fact so clearly that they do not advise even soprano singers to cultivate coloratura singing unless they have the necessary natural facility to begin with. I think myself, however, that all should endeavour to acquire the maximum agility, even if they do not attempt to sing coloratura in public, simply for the benefits which they will derive from it in other respects. After all the voice cannot be possessed of two much flexibility whatever style of music be attempted ; and there is no way in which flexibility can be more surely developed than by the practice of coloratura.

For the rest I can only repeat that, given the right kind of voice in the first place, there is only one way to acquire agility, and that is by practice. No short cuts are possible here, and I have no trade secrets to impart.

And the necessary exercises themselves are all of the simplest character, at all events in the beginning ; just simple scales—or rather portions of scales—in the first instance, with others more elaborate in due course. But the scales are the foundation, and if they are properly mastered the rest will follow without difficulty.

An important feature of good coloratura singing is, of course, not only that the notes shall be cleanly sung, but also that they shall be absolutely in tune and of good tone quality. One not infrequently hears singers who possess the necessary agility to sing the note, but are lacking in these other qualities. Their runs will lack brilliancy because the notes will not be perfectly

HOW TO SING

in tune, and the quality of them will be so hard and disagreeable sometimes as to give more pain than pleasure.

The cause of this will usually have been a desire to make progress too hastily in the earlier stages. They will not have devoted sufficient attention at the outset to practising *slowly*, and so ensuring absolutely just intonation and satisfactory tone quality. Therefore, it is emphatically a case here of " more haste less speed." You cannot acquire velocity quickly. I will not repeat again the well-worn story of Porpora and Caffarelli. But that illustrates the point.

I cannot refrain from adding a few words while on this subject in defence of coloratura, which is so often contemptuously spoken of in these days by those who do not possess the power of singing it. We all know the kind of way in which it is referred to. Coloratura music is false, showy, superficial, unworthy, dramatically unreal, and so on. But what nonsense this is !

What is the difference in principle, I would ask, between the fioriture passages of the vocalist and those introduced as a matter of course in the most serious instrumental music ? Why should a cadenza for the voice be reckoned less worthy than a similar passage for the violin or the 'cello ? All the greatest masters have introduced florid passages in plenty in the noblest instrumental music. Yet the view is very generally adopted that these are inadmissible, or, at all events, belong to an inferior phase of the art when the instrument employed happens to be the voice.

COLORATURA SINGING

No doubt the quality of the works more particularly identified with vocal music of this order has had something to do with the matter. Yet it is hardly necessary to recall that vocal fioriture is by no means confined to the music of Donizetti, Bellini, and the like.

Bach, for one, had no sort of prejudice on the point, as is demonstrated often enough even in his most solemn work, while Handel, again, revelled in coloratura, alike in the case of his operas, containing some of the most wonderful florid music ever written, and of his oratorios, to which no less applied.

That Mozart can be reckoned in the same category it is hardly necessary to recall, while even Beethoven did not disdain to utilise the arts of vocal decoration in many of the numbers of " Fidelio." If, therefore, coloratura singing is sometimes spoken of disrespectfully, it is not from lack of distinguished names which can be cited in its defence.

Nor is it only among the ancients that such are to be found. In the modern Russian School we have Rimsky-Kosakoff's " Hymn to the Sun " from " Coq d'Or." And have we not also such an eminently serious master as Richard Strauss challenging comparison in our own time with the most extravagant productions of the past in this particular genre in the music of Zerbinetta in his " Ariadne " ? One of his latest songs " Amor " is purely for coloratura singers.

As to the charge that coloratura in dramatic music is unnatural and undramatic, those who argue thus surely overlook the fact that all opera might with equal justice be disposed of in the same manner. People do not express themselves in song in real life, any more than they speak in blank verse, as they are made to do in Shakespearean drama.

Yet we are glad to have " Don Giovanni " and " King Lear " none the less ! It is, indeed, truly straining at a gnat and swallowing a camel to condemn coloratura while accepting opera as a whole.

I go further than this, for I venture to say that coloratura can be not only delightful to the ear but also thoroughly appropriate and dramatically expressive. What could be more suitable to give expression to the madness of Lucia than the roulades which Donizetti gives to her ? Or how could the joy of Marguérite be more exquisitely expressed than in the strains of Gounod's Jewel Song ?

I might point in this connection, did modesty permit it, to what people have been good enough to say concerning my own treatment of coloratura in " La Traviata " and elsewhere. I recall that when I first appeared in London it was upon this point particularly that all my critics dwelt.

They were all more especially struck by the manner in which I managed while singing Verdi's florid music brilliantly and effectively in the purely vocal sense, at the same time to make it expressive ; and this I took as the greatest possible compliment which could be bestowed on me. For that I think is what coloratura properly sung should be.

COLORATURA SINGING

It should please the ear by its brilliance, but at the same time it should not, and need not, obscure the dramatic significance of what is sung. I might on this point quote that great artist once again, Lilli Lehmann, who, notwithstanding her strong leaning to music of the more serious class, including Wagner, in which she was so wonderful, was yet a great coloratura singer herself in her younger days, and who has strongly insisted upon the possibility of making even the most florid music expressive also when it is sung in the right way.

She writes : " Thus in the coloratura passages of Mozart's arias I have always sought to gain expressiveness by *crescendi*, choice of significant points for breathing, and breaking off of phrases. I have been especially successful with this in the ' Entführung,' introducing a tone of lament in the first aria, a heroic dignity into the second, through the coloratura passages."

But happily I do not think there is any likelihood of coloratura ever going out of fashion, whatever its detractors may say, so long, at all events, as singers shall be forthcoming who are capable of responding to its demands.

CHAPTER XIX

AFTER the fundamental problems of breathing, tone production and so forth have been dealt with, there is nothing to which the student should pay greater attention than the question of diction, or right enunciation. Yet I am afraid it is rare to find that this view of the matter is acted upon. On the contrary, this question of diction appears to be one of the last to which most singers are disposed to give any serious attention.

Hence the unintelligible sounds which are so often heard proceeding from vocalists alike in the concert room and on the stage, so that one sometimes can scarcely tell even in what language they are supposed to be singing.

This is, of course, a deplorable state of affairs, but yet one so well established that in nine cases out of ten it is hardly thought worthy of remark by the average hearer. It is taken as a matter of course, in other words, that only a word or two, here and there, of those sung shall be understood by the audience, and one may listen attentively to an entire opera without having more than a vague idea at the end as to what it was all about.

ENUNCIATION

Yet in the case of certain singers one may understand without difficulty practically every word they sing, the fact being thereby demonstrated that there is not the slightest real necessity for the incredibly slovenly and defective enunciation which is permitted with such surprising and lamentable tolerance by the public at large.

So far as opera is concerned, I think that the blame rests largely with the managers. If they would adopt the practice of deputing some trustworthy representative at every rehearsal to sit in the topmost gallery and relentlessly pull up every singer whose words could not be clearly understood, the difficulty, I am convinced, would speedily disappear. And operatic directors, I am sure, would find it greatly to their advantage to adopt this course if only on account of the greater popularity which opera would enjoy if it could always be followed, as it should be, as easily as a spoken play.

I believe that in England especially, where opera in the native language is, as I am delighted to see, making such steady headway, its acceptance by the general public is hindered more on this account than by any other reason. Yet there is not the slightest necessity for the presentation of the drama, which is sung instead of being spoken, to be hampered and handicapped in this grievous fashion, and it only needs more vigorous action on the part of the directing powers, I am persuaded, to remedy matters.

So long, however, as singers are left to themselves

in this respect, the difficulty will always remain, since their inevitable tendency is to sacrifice diction to tone quality—in other words, to achieve the best effects in the purely vocal sense and let the words look after themselves.

And this brings us at once to the root of the diction problem, namely, the undoubted difficulty which presents itself at times in reconciling the claims of good tone and clear enunciation. When a pupil is studying he practises upon the easiest vowel sounds and syllables which can be selected ; and many singers, I am afraid, would like nothing better than to be allowed to continue singing upon these agreeable and grateful vocables to the end of their day.

Unfortunately, however, this is not quite possible, and so too many try to get over the difficulty by singing the words not in the way in which they should be pronounced, but in the manner most convenient to themselves. It is hardly necessary to say that this is all wrong and most inartistic, besides being quite unnecessary.

It may be said that it is easy for an Italian to speak thus, and it must certainly be agreed that we Italians are greatly favoured in having the most vocal and melodious of all languages to sing. With our open vowels we may be considered, indeed, to have every advantage in this respect, just as the Germans with their multiplicity of harsh and difficult and, to Italian ears, almost impossible consonants, have every disadvantage.

ENUNCIATION

Yet the principle remains unaffected that every singer, in whatever language, who wishes to be considered a master of his art must contrive to reconcile the claims of good tone with those of accurate and intelligible diction, and the student cannot pay too much attention to this matter from the very moment that he begins to clothe his tones in words.

" Sing as you speak " is a saying which I have heard ascribed to that great master, Jean de Reszke, and though the advice cannot, perhaps, be taken quite literally, it certainly indicates the ideal to be kept in view. It is not feasible to obey the injunction quite literally because it is almost physically impossible to sing certain sounds on certain notes. On this account many teachers—Lamperti himself was one of them—sanction the deliberate modification of the proper vowel sounds or, preferably, the substitution of a more convenient word. But the object should certainly be to keep as near as may be practicable to the correct, natural pronunciation, whereas some seem to make it their aim almost to depart from this as far as possible.

One of the worst examples of execrable enunciation was given by one singer when giving an otherwise creditable rendering of Maude Valerie White's " Devout Lover." The words intended were " Burn at her altar," which were given " Burnateralter."

Some English singers have the habit of putting a vowel after a consonant, as in the word " Goodbye," which becomes " Goodabye " and which is absurd.

Baritones often have a habit of emphasising wrong words, of which one of the best examples is " Trumpeter, what *are* you sounding now ? " Another absurdity.

One could multiply these examples indefinitely.

CHAPTER XX

" ITALIAN is the easiest language to sing, then comes Russian, and I should put English next. All languages affect the tone, unless the tone is first able to carry the weight of the language. A singer may study in any language, but in only one until after the tone is placed beyond any possibility of being affected by the demands of the different languages."

I am disposed to think that there is a good deal of truth in this. How serious is the influence exercised by the language used upon the quality of the tone produced is illustrated by German vocalism and American intonation. For here you have entire nations who, in the vocal sense, may be said to illustrate the evil effect upon tone of a harsh and nasal language.

German singing seems to be different, not merely in degree, but even in kind from that of other lands. In the case of even its best exponents there is a harshness and a tonelessness about it which differentiates it from that of any other race. German singers often have strong, lusty voices, likewise plenty of

79

intelligence and dramatic feeling ; but for beauty of tone and all the finer qualities of vocalism one listens to them in vain.

The fact is strange, but it can hardly be denied even by those least disposed to admit it. That one of the most musical nations in Europe should also be that of all others least dowered with the gift of song is a remarkable paradox which is not a little difficult to understand.

It is not a case of differences of taste. The point is that the German voice, as such, is indisputably inferior in point of quality to that of practically all the other European races. There is no discredit in the circumstance. It implies no reflection on anyone. It is merely an unfortunate physiological fact which must be accepted like any other of those decrees of Nature which are not to be gainsaid.

Such being the fact, how is it to be explained ? Why is it that German singing is of this strange quality ? How has it come about that so musical a race has been so shabbily treated by Nature in this important regard ?

Various theories have been advanced. According to some the explanation is that it is the German language with its explosive consonants, harsh gutturals, and other unmelodious characteristics, which is at the bottom of the trouble.

Students of voice production will prove to you by ingenious experiments that the disposition of the vocal organs, breathing, and so forth, required for the

LANGUAGE

utterance of the German language, are in themselves incompatible with the emission of a beautiful quality of vocal tone ; and however this may be, it is certainly hardly to be disputed that regarded from the standpoint of euphony, pure and simple, the German language is certainly not to be called melodious.

It seems quite a plausible theory, therefore, that harshness of language and harshness of voice are not disconnected, especially when the suggestion is fortified by the converse association of the most beautiful voices with the most mellifluous language, in the case of the Italians.

And if so much be admitted, it is obvious that it may indeed be a question of importance, as Signor Bonci has suggested, what language is employed by the student in that critical initial stage when his voice is being " placed."

For the rest it may be noticed that another great modern tenor, namely Caruso, insisted especially, when discussing this question of placing, upon the supreme necessity of freedom and ease and the absence of all unnecessary contractions of the muscles.

Signor Fugito tells us that on this point he expressed himself as follows : " It is necessary through the aid of self-study and the help of a good singing teacher to become aware of every physical defect—such as contractions of the muscles of the throat, of the face, or of the jaw—which can hinder the tone from being emitted in all its fullness and purity. These rigid muscular contractions bring about a throaty tone, which lacks support and is incapable of purity and amplitude. . . . The singer should apply himself to his study with great naturalness and relaxation ; this is the *sine qua non* of beautiful cantilena singing."

With every word of these remarks I heartily agree. Indeed, I imagine that they would gain the universal assent of all qualified to write on the subject.

The pronunciation of foreign languages is a point to which the student can hardly give too much attention. It also affords another argument in favour of study abroad, since it is certain that a foreign language cannot possibly be acquired so effectually anywhere as in the land where it is spoken. And foreign languages are indispensable to a singer nowadays who aspires to be equal to all the requirements of the modern répertoire.

True it may not be necessary to possess the linguistic powers of a Mingotti, who spoke German, French, Italian, English, and Spanish. But at least it may be laid down as an inexorable rule that no one should ever attempt to sing in a foreign tongue until he has acquired absolute command over every detail of its pronunciation by means of study, if not in the land itself, at any rate with a native.

Otherwise the result can only be a travesty of the composer's—or at all events of the poet's—intentions and a source of mirth to all hearers. Little do some artists realise, indeed, the impressions which they produce at times when, with misplaced assurance, they venture on songs in tongues with which they are imperfectly acquainted.

Even in the case of the best equipped it is a proceeding attended with risk to sing in a foreign language; but without complete knowledge there is no more certain way of exposing one's self to ridicule.

And I am afraid that it must be said that, contrary perhaps to the general belief, Italian suffers no less than any other language from misguided attempts of this kind. The idea is commonly entertained that Italian is " easy " to speak, but of course this is not the case if it is really to be properly spoken.

To which I may add that few peoples seem to experience more difficulty in mastering its subtleties than the English. It may be recalled, too, that this was also the view of Lamperti. Of all the European nations, he declared, the English, and especially Londoners, pronounced Italian worst. The sounds that they produce, he remarked, are nearly all guttural, the vowels being excessively weak, while their accent was entirely wrong—the men, he added, being even worse than the women.

The Scotch, on the other hand, were not quite so bad in his judgment, while the Irish were best of all. Indeed, he agreed that the latter with study could learn to speak Italian quite wonderfully—as is illustrated, I may say, at the present time by Mr. John McCormack, who has a most admirable Italian diction. But it certainly is not often that one can speak in similar terms of the average English artist.

HOW TO SING

If anyone doubts this, let him read and ponder over some caustic remarks once made on this very point by the late Sir Charles Santley. Nothing was more deplorable, he said, than to hear the atrocious manner in which the beautiful Italian language was murdered at times by untrained English singers, and if, he added, they had any notion of the effect which they produced by such attempts upon such of their hearers as happened to be really familiar with the language, they would assuredly never make themselves so ridiculous again. Better a thousand times, he concluded, to sing all your life in your own tongue rather than make yourself a laughing-stock by attempting a task beyond your power.

To which I need hardly add that the same applies no less to French and German, though I am myself less qualified to speak concerning those languages.

It is not for me, perhaps, to say much about Wagner singing, which is so far removed from my own chosen province, but I may be permitted, perhaps, while on the subject of diction, to point to the appalling manner in which the divine art of singing has been perverted by Wagnerian singers under the mistaken notion that they were in this way carrying out the wishes of the sublime master.

I say " under the mistaken notion " because it is well known by those acquainted with the fact that the so-called " Bayreuth method " was as far removed as possible from Wagner's actual ideas. It is true that he attached the utmost importance to clear and

LANGUAGE

emphatic enunciation of the words so that the course of the drama might be quite clearly understood, and therein he was quite right. But there is little reason to suppose that he was in reality satisfied with the actual results achieved by the German singers by whom his works were originally presented.

It is, indeed, an utter mistake to suppose that the harsh and strident singing of the average German vocalist was of a kind to commend itself to Wagner. On the contrary, it was one of his pet schemes, if I have not been misinformed, in connection with Bayreuth, to institute a School of Singing which might lead to better things ; and the kind of singing at which he aimed may be gathered from the fact that the teacher whom he wished to secure to carry out his views was none other than that famous exponent of Bel Canto, the late Señor Manuel Garcia !

In the same connection, too, may be recalled the remark made by the composer after hearing a performance of " Lohengrin " (with the great Italian Wagnerian tenor Borgatti) on one occasion at Bologna. Almost for the first time, he said, he had heard his music really sung. All of which suggests how far they are from actually fulfilling the wishes of the master in continuing at Bayreuth the horrible vocal methods which had become so unfortunately associated with his name.

CHAPTER XXI

D ICTION, it may be said, is included in Style ;
but Style means a good deal more than
diction.

Style may be said, indeed, to mean everything that
the singer adds to the bare notes and directions of the
printed page. These notes and directions are admit-
tedly incomplete—a mere approximation to the
composer's complete meaning. He supplies in this
way the bare facts with such additional hints as to
expression and interpretation as an imperfect system
of notation allows. It is the duty of his interpreters to
supply what is missing—to breathe the spirit of life
into the dry bones and to convert dead printed notes
into living human music.

To this end the singer must possess first of all the
requisite insight and understanding to grasp the
composer's purpose, next the personality and magnetism to be able to realise it for his hearers, and lastly
the musical taste and knowledge required in order to
present it in conformity with the appropriate rules
and traditions. In other words, the singer must not
merely sing the right notes, but sing them in the right

way—with the right accent, the right phrasing, and in the right manner.

What is required may be best realised, perhaps, by comparing the delivery of a fine piece of poetry by a schoolgirl or schoolboy, say, with the delivery of the same lines by an accomplished actor or elocutionist. The words will be the same in both cases, but what a difference in the result ! So in the case of music the notes sung will be the same whoever sings them, but the effect will be vastly different when they are sung by the trained artist.

Here it is that the student's general culture will bear fruit, in the imaginative insight and understanding, the good taste and the expression, which he brings to his task. And here, too, will his musical knowledge and intelligence be more particularly illustrated by the manner in which he conforms to the requirements of the particular kind of music which he is interpreting. For to do this aright a knowledge of the notes alone will not suffice.

He must be familiar also with the varying needs of the different schools of music, with the historical traditions associated with them, and so forth. Opera demands one kind of singing, oratorio another, German *Lieder* another, and so on throughout ; and each of these general classifications can be subdivided in turn.

How different are the requirements of each is best exemplified by the fact that so few succeed in all. One singer will be great in opera, another in oratorio,

HOW TO SING

a third in *Lieder* ; but only in the rarest instances will you find one and the same artist excelling in all. Why is this ? Simply because their respective requirements are so different.

For this reason the average artist will, I think, usually be well advised to confine himself to the class of work more particularly suited to his talent. While it is well to cultivate versatility so far as possible, it is a mistake to sing music of a kind for which you are not suited. Patti loved Wagner, for instance, and was a frequent visitor to Bayreuth. But she did not sing his music. She liked to hear it sung by others, but she realised that it was not for her. Voice, personality, training, temperament, all impose necessary limitations.

People blame me sometimes, for instance, for confining myself mainly to music of a certain school. But I think I know best as to this, and that I am exercising sound judgment in adopting this course. There is much music which I admire and love, but I do not always try to sing it. In the same way I may admire frocks which I see on other women, but I do not necessarily try to wear the same myself. I have the good sense to recognise that they would not suit me.

Moreover, the field of music is so vast that to cultivate one or two departments thoroughly will be more than sufficient to tax the energy of the most ambitious. Make yourself master or mistress in your own chosen province, and you will have accomplished quite as much as anyone need wish to.

STYLE AND INTERPRETATION

And whatever style you cultivate get as near to perfection in it as you can possibly. Catalani said of Sontag : "*Elle est la première dans son genre ; mais son genre n'est pas le premier.*" This may or may not have been true. But Sontag was probably well pleased in any case to be " *la première.*"

CHAPTER XXII

HOW I SING AN ARIA

TO sing a song or a big aria well you must, for the time, be both the vocalist and composer of the words and music you wish to express. If I wish to sing, say, " Home Sweet Home," I must imagine how far I am away from sunny Italy, and forget all the kindness and attention with which I am surrounded here. Then, I begin to feel the mood and homesickness coming to aid me, vocal control must do the rest in making the song effective.

Or, again, if I wish to do justice to Sir Frederick Cowen's charming little song, " The Swallows," I must think of a lovely sunny morning and, mentally, " Open wide my lattice, letting in the laughing breeze," imagining all the joyous sense of life that the arrival of the swallows brings to my naturally vivacious Southern nature.

Let us, however, take the Recitative and Polonaise from that brilliantly sparkling opera " Mignon," by Ambroise Thomas. First of all, I have to study the setting of this great aria, and then, study the words, which, in English begin,

"Yes! for to-night, I am Queen of the Fairies,
And, here my golden sceptre see ;
And behold these, my trophies ! "

HOW I SING AN ARIA

Yes; for to night I am queen of the
fai . . ries' And here my golden sceptre see;
And be- hold . these my tro-phies

I ask myself what I might feel like were I able to
become a fairy. Giving myself free rein, I sing the
whole recitative much as I would speak it, only having in
mind the notes, I attack them firmly, letting the
conductor punctuate the whole with the accompaniment somewhat freely. In recitative, one must have
fire and imagination, and, although reasonable attention must be paid to the valuation of notes—the full
five beats, for example, on the long note of bars 6 and 7
—it is the part of the accompanist to feel your pulse,
as it were, and go with you. Now, on the same long
note, be careful to carry a sense of increasing wonder,
by making a *diminuendo*, then, with increasing verve,
make a clean " turn " on beat four of the 8th bar,
capped by a triumphant pause, and, a clean interval
of the fifth with the word " trophies," on beats one
and two of bar 9.

Now we come to the actual Polacca, in which, *tempo*

91

must be observed and all the tricks of brilliant vocal agility put into play. Remember, all these " runs " and bravura passages must be clear—every note like a fresh pea out of a pod, or bullet out of a machine gun ! Observe the boldness of " picking up " at the beginning of the polacca movement, and in bar 3 of this movement how smoothly the detached notes have to be sung.

Moderato tempo di Polacca (96 = ♩)

Here, again, there must be no scooping up an octave, but a clear rise of the octave, giving the sense of all, as it were, one piece. Thus, " I—I *am* Titania," and repeat the same words with even greater fervour, treating all the words and music with the same mentality, and, as vital to the whole.

Many so-called intellectual singers prefer *Lieder*, because they cannot vocalise the fine, dashing, graceful runs of florid music, not because of its lack of intellectual requirements. What could better express the vivacious joy of a fairy queen than the triplet passages on the exclamation " *Ah !* " bars 14 and 15 of the polacca movement.

HOW I SING AN ARIA

ry! Ah!

When we come to bars 29 and 30, there is the chance of a lifetime with the cadenza-like string of 15 notes, in the neatest sets of three, and they should be as perfect as though played by Kreisler on the violin.

Later on we come to some roulade passages of six notes on the same exclamation " Ah ! " (bars 43, 44, and 45) which must be sung with increasing verve, so

fai - - ry! Ah!

that the wood wind of the orchestra comes running up perfectly in tune and tempo, as it were from right under your last note. Here, much depends upon the cue of the conductor, but, changing one's manner and keeping up the growing joyfulness, you begin a new era, as it were, with the words " Bright troops of fairies

Bright troops of fai_ries ho_ver round me! ___

93

hover round me." Thus, the aria works on, until, on the last beat of bar 54 and bar 55 there is a suggestion of a fairy call. A dream-like waltz, in wide contrast, follows. Unless one feels this, the brilliance we have

worked up is losing the value of contrast with this shimmer, as it were, of gleaming moonlight. On this breaks the brilliant passages of the flute, which may be the task of some fairy worker in the real fairy land ! I must be wafted along in smooth subservience to the brilliance of the accompaniment for the next few bars, until I repeat the lovely melody at bar 62 when I begin to add—as scored in the part—some grace notes and

florid passages, and gradually awaken until, at bar 79, I have ascended to a full top B, preceded by a " trill " or " shake," that leads up to the brilliant burst of the orchestra back to the polacca-like movement, and to the finale. This must be one increasing triumph, over the much talked of top E flat, the roulades, grace

HOW I SING AN ARIA

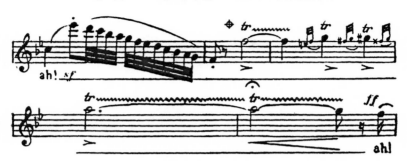

notes, trills, and cadenza-like passages for sheer *joie de vivre.* Yet all this depends upon how well you have conditioned yourself, practised those tiring vowel sounds, scales, sustained passages, to which I commend you before essaying the brilliant Polonaise from "Mignon" that has given me many triumphs, yet still calls for all I can give, as it will to the end of the chapter.

CHAPTER XXIII

PRACTISING

IS it necessary to say that daily practice is indispensable to the student—as it is also to the finished artist ? A celebrated violinist used to say, " If I cease practising for one day I know it when I next play ; if for two days my enemies know it ; if for three the public know it." It is the same with the voice, although some voices, no doubt, require less daily exercising than others.

Some fortunate ones, indeed, have been able to dispense with it almost entirely. On the day of a performance the great Chaliapine warms his voice up for a period of thirty or forty minutes only. On other days and when on vacation he rarely practises, except for getting up new music, and even this is more of a mental process. It is said of Mario also that at the height of his fame he never practised more than ten minutes a day, and that just before he was leaving for the Opera House, while his servant would be standing, watch in hand, assuring him that he would be late for the performance if he did not start at once. But that, of course, was an exceptional case.

PRACTISING

On the other hand, Battistini is most lavish with his practising and rarely a day passes that he does not put in one or two hours of solid singing. This no doubt accounts for the extraordinary command he has over tone, phrasing and breathing. There is great truth in the saying that practice makes perfect, but how many of us have the robust and natural organ that Battistini is blessed with. I always thought that the reason of this was the fact that Battistini, who could well have trained as a tenor, elected to become a baritone, thus evading the strain of forcing high " C's " out of his voice.

At the same time even practising should not be carried to excess. Many singers have, indeed, often done their voices great harm by practising too much. The vocal cords are exceedingly delicate and cannot be used too carefully. There can be no doubt that the wonderful preservation of Patti's voice was due in large measure to the extraordinary prudence and care with which she husbanded it. By never singing at rehearsals, by never singing when she was in the least degree out of health or tired, and so on, she added years probably to the length of her career. And all singers should act as far as possible on the same principle.

There should never be the smallest strain in practising, for instance. For this reason it is advisable to practise with the half voice mostly and only rarely at the extremities of the compass—and then with great care and discretion. In the same way there should never be any sense of fatigue, still less of hoarseness, after practice.

It is, indeed, in the ordinary way a sure sign that something is wrong, either with your vocal organs or with your methods, if this occurs often, and the matter should be investigated accordingly—even to the extent of changing your teacher if necessary.

If, however, the trouble is only temporary, a brief suspension of exercising may be all that is necessary. But in this case be careful not to resume your practising until the trouble has completely disappeared. Far better drop your practising for a week, or a month, if necessary, than attempt to sing when your organs are not in perfect order.

That is to say, if there is really definite trouble. If, on the other hand, it is merely a little hoarseness, such as many singers are subject to, then *judicious* exercising—please notice that I underline judicious— may be the best thing for it. This is, however, essentially a matter upon which you must be guided by your teacher—or even if necessary by a doctor.

Madame Lilli Lehmann prescribes, for instance, what she calls the Great Scale as an invaluable remedy for all manner of vocal ills—meaning simply long slow scales of sustained notes steadily repeated. Here is what she said, for instance, on this point :

The great scale properly employed in practice accomplishes wonders. It equalises the voice, makes it flexible and noble, gives strength to all weak places,

PRACTISING

operates to repair all breaks and faults that exist, and controls the voice to the very heart. Nothing escapes it. It is the Guardian Angel of the voice. I sing it every day, often twice, even if I have to sing one of my greatest rôles in the evening. I can rely absolutely on its assistance.

And, as I have said, she prescribed this very exercise not only for daily practice when one is well, but also as a remedy for troubles when the voice is out of order. I may be permitted, perhaps, to quote in this connection another interesting passage :

I myself had to sing Norma in Vienna some years ago, and got up in the morning quite hoarse. By nine o'clock I tried my invaluable remedy, but could not sing above A flat, although in the evening I should have to reach high D flat and E flat. I was on the point of giving up because the case seemed to be so desperate. Nevertheless, I practised till 11 o'clock, half an hour at a time, and noticed that I was gradually getting better. In the evening I had my D flat and E flat at my command so that people said they had seldom heard me sing so well.

I have quoted this advice of Lilli Lehmann because it is of interest and value as coming from so great an authority, but I do not wish it to be understood that this has been my own precise practice, for this is not the case. But as to the general value of scales for practising purposes there is, of course, no possible doubt. Scales are, indeed, the foundation of all useful practice, especially at first.

HOW TO SING

Marchesi, for instance, relied on them almost exclusively in the earlier stages—long sustained tones, repeated again and again until her fastidious ear was satisfied ; and no pupil can possibly fail to benefit from such exercise. Even for the acquisition of velocity, as I have said elsewhere, scales—and quite slow ones at first—are indispensable.

Of more elaborate exercises there are none better, so far as I know, than those to be found in Concone, while for advanced pupils well-chosen numbers from the great Italian operatic masters, Rossini, Donizetti, Bellini, and the rest, can be utilised with great advantage. This includes mezzo-sopranos, contraltos, as well as sopranos. My maestro would make them all sing " Una voce poco fa " transposed, saying that it was a vocal massage.

But it is rather a matter for the individual teacher to prescribe what is required in this way, since all voices will not need the same.

As to the period and duration of practising, my own plan is to practise twice a day—at ten in the morning for an hour, with intervals of rest ; and again in the afternoon, before dinner, for the same time. But the beginner should not practise for more than ten or fifteen minutes at a time, and should leave off immediately his voice begins to feel tired.

To which, I would add, that it is of the utmost importance not only what one practises but *how*. Ten minutes' practice with the maximum of thought and concentration will be of more value than a whole

PRACTISING

hour of mere mechanical scales and arpeggi, sung without thought and care.

The pupil, while practising, should listen to himself with the utmost vigilance all the time—criticising ruthlessly every tone, and seeking always to eradicate every fault and blemish. It is for lack of this *mental* effort that pupils so often practise in vain—improving themselves in certain respects perhaps, but never acquiring that beauty of tone and perfection of execution which should be the foundation of all.

I would repeat here, indeed, what I have said before, that unsparing self-criticism is the root of all progress. Nor should this ever cease. As a great artist remarked in some words which I quoted earlier, the true artist will continue studying and practising and improving to the end of his day.

Read, for instance, what Signor Fucito tells us of Caruso :

No one could have been a severer critic of Caruso's art than Caruso himself. He worked with tremendous concentration, and his acute ear was ever ready to descry the slightest flaw in the tone production, in quality or the interpretation of a musical passage.

And again :

There were times when he refused to rest, singing a passage or phrase over and over again, each time with another vocal modulation of colouring until he got the expression and quality that satisfied his exacting musical taste.

HOW TO SING

It is interesting to note, by the way, that Caruso practised always, or nearly always, with the full voice —a procedure which is not, however, as I have already said, to be generally recommended.

Incidentally in practising the student should avoid the acquisition of bad habits of standing, undesirable movements with the hands, and so on, and should also keep careful check upon his facial expressions. For the latter purpose it is an excellent plan to practise before a mirror, since this is the surest way to avoid the unconscious cultivation of undesirable tricks which, once they have been acquired, may prove most difficult to get rid of.

In the case of operatic artists it is a good plan also to practise in costume in order to become accustomed to the dress which one will be wearing in the actual performance, and thus to avoid any sense of awkwardness which may be otherwise experienced. And for the same reason when any particular number has to be sung in any special manner from the physical point of view, as, for instance, sitting down, or kneeling, it is well to become accustomed to this also beforehand.

CHAPTER XXIV

THE ARTIST AND THE GRAMOPHONE

BEFORE leaving the subject of practising I should like to add a word as to the value of the gramophone to the intelligent student. This is, indeed, a truly invaluable adjunct. If to hear the greatest singers is the finest of all experiences for the student, how can it indeed be otherwise ? For here in the most convenient manner possible is the means provided for doing this. In the earlier pages of this volume I have recorded what inestimable advantages I derived in my own case from the constant hearing of fine singing from my earliest childhood. Now, by means of the gramophone, the same advantage is at the command of everyone wheresoever he, or she, may happen to reside.

In my younger days only those dwelling in the great capitals could hope to hear such artists as Patti, Tamagno, Caruso, Battistini, and so forth, and even those only if means permitted, which was not often in the case of poor students.

To-day anyone can enjoy this priceless privilege, wherever he may happen to reside, for a comparatively small outlay through the agency of the gramophone.

HOW TO SING

And he can hear them not only now and again, but as often as ever he likes and by his own fireside. If he happens to be studying some particular rôle he can be " coached " in this most practical and unrivalled manner by all the greatest artists of the day. He can take a particular aria and hear it sung by Caruso again and again until he is familiar with every detail of his rendering—can note his breathing, his phrasing, and every other detail in a manner which would be quite impossible by any other means.

And having heard Caruso he can then hear the same number sung by various other great artists if he chooses, and benefit still more by comparing their respective readings—by noting how they resemble one another or how they differ, as the case may be, incidentally learning in the process how widely one interpretation may differ from another and still be of the highest order.

Not only this, but he can familiarise himself with entire operas in the same way, for certain of the companies issue complete albums of the best known works which are reproduced in their entirety—vocal parts, orchestra, and all in this marvellous manner. One would think, indeed, that the coming generation should provide us with fine singers in such plenty as the world has never known before with the aid of such priceless help.

Whether it will be so or not, remains to be seen. But certainly it may be said that never before have students been so wonderfully helped. I myself have pleasure in testifying that I have derived the greatest benefit as well as delight from the records of Patti, while Mr. John McCormack has similarly acknowledged his indebtedness to the wonderful renderings of Caruso.

And I hope in all modesty that students of the present generation may derive similar help in turn from the records which I myself have made. Beyond a doubt the gramophone should be the guide, philosopher, and friend—the most trusted and most competent aid and coadjutor—not only to every student, but also to every teacher of the present day.

Of course, the pupil is only human and often reluctant to believe that there are grave faults in his voice. Whilst others can detect his mistakes, the pupil cannot listen intelligently to his own faulty emission while singing.

But take him to a recording-room and get him to sing into the recording-horn, and let him listen as the operator tries over the record he has made. He is sure to be surprised to find how many faults there are.

His production may be throaty, nasal, or what you will. It is all brought out clearly by the gramophone.

There is no instrument that is so calculated to remove the conceit from a young artist as the gramophone. To watch his face as he first listens to his own voice is usually to enjoy a miniature pantomime.

Nevertheless, the gramophone is a spur to drive the artist forward to perfection, and, of course, a great aid to the music professor.

CHAPTER XXV

DIFFERENT artists have different methods of studying their parts, but all I think will be agreed on one point, namely, that they cannot possibly be learned too thoroughly. Marvellous stories are told, no doubt, of difficult rôles having been completely mastered by prodigious efforts in a fabulously short time. But he is taking terrible risks who attempts a *tour de force* of this kind, and in my own opinion no artist should ever be asked to do this. To master a rôle in the proper way should be a matter of weeks and months, not to say years, of careful study so that it becomes part and parcel, as it were, of the very being of the artist. Then, and then only, can it be attempted on the stage with that absolute confidence and assurance and that entire freedom from anxiety without which the best results cannot possibly be hoped for.

Very foolish, or at all events very courageous, is the young artist who for the sake of an appearance at all costs essays a part which he, or she, has not thoroughly prepared beforehand—for that way disaster lies. A part simply cannot be too well studied if failure and mishaps are to be absolutely assured against.

HOW TO SING

Let it be remembered especially by the student who runs through a part so easily in the privacy of his study with the aid of a friendly accompanist at the piano, how infinitely more difficult are the conditions on the actual stage—alike in the psychological and purely material senses.

There is the consciousness, in the first place, of being part now of a huge inexorable organisation which admits of no error or failure under any circumstances, and that at first has an almost paralysing effect upon the faculties. There is the consciousness of that eager, critical public on the other side of the footlights and of all that there is at stake should any failure occur. There is the difficulty in the physical sense of hearing the orchestra properly, which seems so far off and so infinitely less helpful than the friendly homely piano. There are the perturbing factors of one's costume, action, business. In short, the whole thing is utterly different, and for this reason, therefore, the young artist cannot be too firmly grounded in his rôle if he is to be proof against all the possibilities of failure and all mischances and mishaps in the hour of trial.

As to the actual process of mastering a rôle I believe thoroughly in the practice of studying it at the outset apart from the music. Read the whole book through and master the story and the drama completely in the first instance. Get every twist and turn and every detail of it into your mind. Try to visualise and represent it to yourself as realistically as possible.

Imagine that it all actually occurred and that you

STUDYING A RÔLE

were, in fact, the character whose part you are to represent. Learn all you can about the period of the story, the scene of the action, the circumstances of the time, and so on, so as to realise it all as vividly as possible.

And then, having done this, study with equal thoroughness every detail of your own part. It may be only a small one. Never mind. You can make it just as lifelike and as perfect in its way as one of more importance if you make the most of it.

It was in this way that Mario always studied his parts, and most other great artists, I think, will be found to adopt a similar method. We read of Mario that no trouble was too great and no research too laborious to ensure that any rôle which he had undertaken should be represented as correctly and as perfectly as possible. Nor did his fastidious care end there, for he paid the greatest attention to his words also and even re-wrote every line of his part in Gounod's "Faust" because the words of the original Italian version were not sufficiently singable to please him.

It was Mario, also, who said that unless he had all that he was singing about in his head as well as in his throat he could never hope to do justice to his part.

It is the old, old story. The greatest results in anything are only to be attained by unsparing labour. It may not be a complete statement of the case to say that genius is only an infinite capacity for taking pains. But it is certainly true to say that that capacity is almost always associated with the highest genius.

HOW TO SING

Caruso supplied a more recent instance. He took endless pains to get his parts right in every detail. He was as careful, we read, about creating the proper make-up for the character which he was impersonating as he was about studying the proper gestures, declamation, and musical expression.

Signor Fucito writes :

He pondered the mental, emotional and moral traits of the character as they were revealed not only in his own lines and music, but throughout the entire opera. If he found that insufficient he searched elsewhere—in art, in literature, in history. When he was preparing the rôle of Samson he went to the Bible for additional enlightenment on that legendary hero in order that he might visualise him more vividly; and when he was studying Eleazar he sought advice on Jewish customs from a prominent Yiddish actor of New York.

Respecting " make-up " this should be done as carefully and artistically as possible, bearing in mind always that although some of the audience may be a long way off, others will be much nearer, while opera glasses will further help to abridge the distance and to reveal every detail.

CHAPTER XXVI

CHOICE OF DEBUT WORK

A S regards the choice of opera for debut purposes I need hardly say that this is a matter of great importance which should be most carefully considered. If you happen to be exceptionally gifted and possess the advantage of powerful connections you may perhaps be able to appear at once in a rôle of the first importance, but my opinion is that it is usually much better to begin with smaller parts and acquire the necessary stage experience before attempting one of the more exacting rôles.

You may, of course, have such natural gifts and be so well trained and coached for the purpose that you may achieve success at a bound, but the chances are against this, and it is much more likely that you will fall short of your expectations and thereby imperil your career at the outset by making a false start. *C'est le premier pas*, etc., and it is much better to begin modestly and learn your business thoroughly before attempting the higher flights. Then when you are properly qualified and have acquired the necessary experience you can take a more important part with the assurance that you will be able at least to do full justice to yourself and to make the utmost of your natural powers.

There is another reason, too, why it is a mistake, as a rule, to attempt the heavier rôles too soon—namely, the fact that the voice and the general physique, apart from the question of training and experience, are seldom ready for these at first. I have, indeed, known more than one case in which a career of promise has been ruined after a brilliant start by subjecting a young singer too soon to the heavy strain of the most important parts.

Study these rôles by all means and have them ready —or one or two of them—in case some exceptional or unexpected opportunity should present itself. But do not be in too great a hurry to appear in them. It is a much safer course, as a rule, to make good at first in those of a less ambitious kind ; and you need never be afraid that good work in these will go unnoticed or unrewarded. But whichever part you choose for the purpose it should naturally be one which is well suited to your capacity and in which you are confident of being able to do your best.

If the novice can attach himself or herself to some provincial opera company at a nominal salary for the purpose of training and experience, this is often a good plan. In Italy almost every provincial city has a small season of opera, and impresarios in most cases are ready to give a promising singer a debut without pay in order to reduce their expenses. But in some instances if a singer desires to make a debut in a certain rôle and imposes this on the impresario she will be required to help to finance the opera by the payment of a few thousand lire. This is often done, but in some instances with sad results, because it is usually an indifferent artist who forces a début in this way, often against the better judgment of the manager.

I have known instances, indeed, where a singer has obtained a debut on these terms, and the audience, after hearing the singer, has protested so vigorously that the unfortunate novice has had to be withdrawn in favour of a more satisfactory substitute in order to pacify the public.

In one instance I remember a Canadian tenor of tremendous size, but with a voice more like a mad bull's than that of a human being, who thought he would make an ideal Othello. He was wealthy and paid the management 25,000 lire for a debut. After the first act such a commotion was created in the theatre that the carabinieri had to step in and decide that either the show should be stopped or else continued by another artist.

Shortly afterwards columns appeared in the American papers about the harsh treatment of foreign singers in Italy. I can only say, however, that in my judgment it is utterly wrong to force on the public artists who are manifestly incapable, and that in this particular case the punishment fitted the crime !

In cases where there really are voice and merit such

HOW TO SING

methods should be quite unnecessary, since managers are only too eager to secure fresh talent and to offer suitable opportunities for appearing before the public to those who possess it.

Just another suggestion. Don't be induced to accept a dramatic rôle if your voice is purely lyric. Don't even be tempted. Certain *maestri* are always looking for voices that can be heard above their orchestras. They never find one, because it doesn't exist; but the path of their search is strewn with wrecked voices.

CHAPTER XXVII

REHEARSALS

REHEARSALS are a necessary evil and the sensible artist will try to make the best of them. Undoubtedly they are very tedious and trying, but they are quite unavoidable unless you happen to have attained sufficient eminence to be dispensed attendance at them. And even then it is not always wise to avoid them if you wish to procure the best results.

Patti, throughout the greater part of her career, never attended any rehearsals. But then she always sang in the best-known operas with thoroughly experienced fellow-artists who were carefully instructed as to her requirements. But it is hardly necessary to say that her case was exceptional.

Some artists are very trying at rehearsals by coming with their parts imperfectly prepared, by arriving late, and so on, and in such cases the company in general is fortunate if the manager is sufficiently firm to insist on proper discipline being observed.

A strict conductor who allows no trifling of this kind is, indeed, the truest friend of the artists, and his authority should be recognised accordingly by one and all. It is of the utmost importance that artists should be thoroughly acquainted with their parts, and they should take advantage of rehearsals to master every detail of their action, business, and so on, leaving absolutely nothing to chance.

There is, however, no need to sing with full voice at rehearsals ; indeed, this is not desirable. But one should naturally sing loud enough to indicate quite clearly one's intentions. Nor should the inexperienced artist show any reluctance to take advice from the stage manager when it is given. For his judgment will probably be better than yours, and in any case it is your business to do as he directs.

CHAPTER XXVIII

CONTRACTS

IN the case of young singers with very promising voices, impresarios are often found who are willing to finance the period of instruction for a term of say five years. Their calculations are that in the last few years of this period the artist will become a profitable investment for them.

In the case of a poor artist this is often a very good plan, since it is to the interest of the impresario to assist in making a name and a position for the artist as well as in seeing that he has a proper training. And the latter may easily find himself the gainer by the arrangement therefore.

Speaking generally, however, I am not very much in favour of such contracts, for the simple reason that the career of an artist being so short he ought not to be placed in the position of expending his powers for the benefit of another person. I have known artists drawing £100 a performance who were receiving a mere £10 a week under such an agreement as I have described ; and this is, of course, a very unsatisfactory and even heart-breaking state of things.

Caruso was one, it will be remembered, who entered

into such a contract as a student which, however, he finally succeeded in getting rescinded, though not before he had had recourse to the Law Courts for this purpose.

As to contracts made later, when a proper position has been secured, the artist will not usually need much advice regarding these, since he is generally quite able to look after himself. " Too well, indeed," it is sometimes said, by directors and managers.

Yet it must be remembered that, as noted above, the vocalist's career is usually very brief. The years of gain may be from five to twenty, but are rarely much more than ten. I have known great artists who have lasted for but a few seasons. On the other hand, I can recall some like Battistini who have had over forty years of lucrative employment. But this is very rare.

Are they not justified, therefore, in requiring generous payment while they can obtain it ? Also it must be remembered that great singers are exceptionally endowed, and as such are entitled to demand exceptional rewards. In which connection one may recall the famous reply of the dancer Gabrielli to the Empress Catherine of Russia. The Empress was staggered by the terms which she demanded, and declared that not even her Field-Marshals received so much. Whereupon Gabrielli recommended the Empress to get her Marshals to dance for her.

Some of the most exacting contracts ever made by a singer were, I suppose, those of Catalani. In her agreements when she was singing in London she used to stipulate for half of the receipts throughout the entire season, while she inserted further such conditions as the following : " Madame Catalani shall choose and direct the operas which she is to sing ; she shall likewise have the choice of the performers in them ; and she will have no orders to receive from anyone."

Madame Patti in turn received as much as £1000 a performance from Mapleson in America. But then Patti was—Patti ! Most artists are content with less ! And to such I would say as my final word on this point : " Do not forget during the days of your necessarily brief prosperity to make provision at all costs for the future."

CHAPTER XXIX

IF I have spoken largely about opera in these pages, this is because with my experience it comes most naturally to me to do this. But concert work—of which also I have done my share—is of course equally important, and a few words on this subject may not come amiss therefore.

It is hardly necessary to say that the kind of singing which is suitable for the stage is not always equally in keeping on the platform. It is the difference here between acting and recitation.

On the stage you are actually impersonating the character you represent, and the fullest amount of realism is therefore permissible—indeed, essential. On the platform the same amount of licence is not allowable. You are here not impersonating, but interpreting at one remove, so to speak.

You are not pretending to represent the actual character of the song ; you are reproducing in *your own personality* the feelings and emotions involved. Or as one might put it, the art of the stage is representative ; that of the concert platform is reproductive.

All this must be borne in mind, therefore, by the

artist who turns from the stage to the concert room. The effect produced may be just as great, but it must be achieved in a different way—without action, without gesture even, but with the maximum of intensity none the less—secured by means of the voice, the expressiveness of the singing and the personality and temperament of the singer alone.

And these will be all sufficient for those who know their business ; nor should they be exceeded in the ordinary way. Yet if it comes naturally to you to go a little further now and again, I do not know that it need be condemned.

Observe, however, that I say " if it comes naturally to you." Otherwise, it will be forced and theatrical, and will certainly not achieve its purpose. It is purely a question of temperament. Be natural and spontaneous and you will not go far astray. Northern peoples indulge sparingly in gestures on the concert platform, but yet get great results without their aid.

We Latin races are less restrained in this respect because this is in accordance with our natural temperaments. It is the difference between one who gesticulates freely in ordinary speech and one who never stirs a finger. One would not counsel the Englishman to copy the foreigner's gestures for it would not come naturally to him to do this ; but one would not have a Frenchman or an Italian without them.

And so it is in singing. If an occasional gesture comes naturally to you there is no need to repress it, even if you cannot be recommended to go as far in this

HOW TO SING

respect in the concert room as Jenny Lind did on one occasion if report may be trusted. It is recorded that once when singing Agathe's prayer from " Der Freischütz " at a concert at Norwich she was so carried away that she actually fell on her knees on the platform and so finished the air ! That was, perhaps, overdoing things. Certainly I have never heard of even an Italian concert-singer going quite so far.

I need hardly add, while on the subject of concert deportment, that a pleasing and ingratiating manner is also much to be desired, though this is a matter that seems to be strangely overlooked too often by young artists of the present day. One might think almost from the manners of some of them that they consider themselves to be conferring the greatest possible favour upon their hearers by condescending to sing to them.

And doubtless in many cases they actually do think this ! But they should endeavour not to indicate the fact quite so clearly by their demeanour. I have seen artists of this self-sufficient type who actually make not the slightest response, or barely any, when an audience is good enough to applaud them ! This sort of thing is quite incomprehensible to me, and I am sure that if those who behave thus had any conception of the impression which they produce they would speedily mend their manners.

CHAPTER XXX

HEALTH, DIET, ETC.

GOOD health is essential to a singer, and it must be most carefully preserved. To this end one should live as wholesome and regular an existence as possible, seeing that you get plenty of fresh air and taking such exercise as may be found convenient, but without overdoing things in the latter respect, since undue muscular exertion is sometimes prejudicial.

Moderation in diet is also advisable, avoiding especially all highly seasoned dishes, pepper, pickles, and the like, and in the matter of alcohol, if this be taken, confining one's self to the lightest kinds of wines·

As for smoking I prohibit it entirely, as I conside it to be the greatest enemy of the vocal cords, although I am well aware, of course, that some of the most famous singers have been inveterate smokers.

Of Mario, for instance, we are told that he was never seen without a cigar in his mouth except when he was eating. He smoked, it is recorded, even in his bath, although it may be noted that even he expressly avoided cigarettes, confining himself exclusively to cigars.

HOW TO SING

Caruso, again, was another tremendous smoker, and I suppose there are few male vocalists, at any rate, who deny themselves in this respect entirely. But I have no doubt that it would be better for their vocal organs if they did so all the same.

Coughs and colds are, of course, the greatest bugbear of the singer, and to assist in securing immunity from these do not allow your throat to become too sensitive by wrapping up too much. Bathing the throat with cold water helps also towards this end. When over-heated and perspiring never delay changing into dry clothes, and be especially careful always to keep the feet dry.

Yet with all the precautions in the world the time will come when concerts or performances must be given under unfavourable conditions, and in these circumstances the art and the courage of the singer alone will carry her through.

Often I have undertaken a concert rather than disappoint the public when suffering from a bad cold. But I have been able by will power to do wonders in these circumstances, and more often than not I have been rewarded by a Press which said that I had never sung better.

I have known Caruso, under such circumstances, the morning before a widely advertised concert, at which an audience of perhaps 10,000 people was likely to be present, to wake up and find himself entirely without voice.

In the instance I have in mind he telegraphed for a

celebrated throat specialist in New York to come immediately to Pittsburg, where just previous to the concert he underwent heroic treatment. This meant the administering of a stimulant to the vocal cords which contracted them for a period of a few hours.

Thereby he was enabled to fulfil his engagement, though the after results put him out of action for at least a week.

A singer cannot hope always to be absolutely at his best, and this fact should be realised from the first by young artists. Frequently, prior to a performance, if the artist cannot bring off certain customary effects he, or she, will be thrown immediately into a state of distraction and despair. This, however, is all wrong.

Engagements must be kept, and more often than not, as I have suggested, the artist will find when the time comes that his apprehension had been quite uncalled for. Strung up by the needs of the case, and making a special call upon all his resources, mental and emotional as well as merely vocal, he will very likely do even better than usual.

He should bear this in mind, therefore, another time, and never lose his head even though he may think that he has lost his voice !

At the same time this is not to say that really serious voice trouble should be ignored, and I myself make it a practice in every large town where I am accustomed to stay for any length of time to learn of a suitable medical man or voice specialist to whom I can repair for advice in case of need.

HOW TO SING

As to one's régime on the day when one is actually singing this merits a few words perhaps. Having gone to bed betimes the day before, so as to secure a long night of unbroken rest, I myself do not usually rise until about ten or eleven, when I have a light breakfast of tea and toast and soft-boiled eggs. For lunch, if one may call it such, after a short walk, I have merely a cup of cocoa and a little fruit, and nothing more until after the concert. Most other artists of my acquaintance do likewise.

Printed in the United Kingdom
by Lightning Source UK Ltd.
130530UK00001B/31/A

9 781846 641282